TC 3-22.23 (FM 23-23)

*Training Circular
No. 3-22.23 (FM 23-23)

Headquarters
Department of the Army
Washington, DC, 15 November 2013

M18A1 CLAYMORE MUNITION

Contents

		Page
	PREFACE	v
Chapter 1	DESCRIPTION, CAPABILITIES, AND COMPONENTS	1-1
	Effects	1-1
	Components	1-1
	Safety	1-3
Chapter 2	METHOD OF INITIATION: SHOCK TUBE ASSEMBLY WITH PULL INITIATOR	2-1
	Section I. Components	2-1
	Shock Tube Assembly With Pull Initiator	2-2
	M7 Bandoleer	2-3
	Section II. Standard Operation	2-4
	Selecting and Preparing a Firing Position	2-5
	Employing	2-6
	Aiming	2-8
	Arming	2-9
	Camouflaging	2-15
	Firing	2-16
	Section III. Operation Under Unusual Conditions	2-18
	Addressing a Misfire	2-18
	Disarming	2-25
	Recovering	2-26
	Destroying	2-27
Chapter 3	METHOD OF INITIATION: M57 FIRING DEVICE	3-1
	Section I. Components	3-1
	M57 Firing Device	3-2
	M4 Electrical Blasting Cap Assembly	3-4
	M40 Test Set	3-5
	M7 Bandoleer	3-6

---

*This publication supersedes FM 23-23, 1 January 1966.

i

Contents

	Section II. Standard Operation	3-7
	Selecting and Preparing a Firing Position	3-7
	Conducting a Circuit Test	3-8
	Employing	3-16
	Aiming	3-20
	Arming	3-21
	Camouflaging	3-24
	Conducting a Final Circuit Test	3-24
	Firing	3-25
	Section III. Operation Under Unusual Conditions	**3-27**
	Addressing a Misfire	3-27
	Disarming	3-28
	Recovering	3-29
	Destroying	3-30
Chapter 4	**TRAINING**	**4-1**
	Phases of Training	4-1
	Sustainment Training	4-2
	Training Aids	4-2
	Instructors/Trainers	4-2
	Training Preparation	4-3
	Range Coordinations	4-5
	Training Conduct	4-7
Chapter 5	**EMPLOYMENT CONSIDERATIONS**	**5-1**
	Uses	5-1
	Fire Discipline	5-2
	Controlled Frontal Coverage	5-2
	Operations	5-3
GLOSSARY		**Glossary-1**
REFERENCES		**References-1**
INDEX		**Index-1**

Figures

Figure 1-1. M18A1 claymore munition 1-1
Figure 1-2. Danger radius and effects of the M18A1 claymore munition 1-4
Figure 2-1. M18A1 claymore munition with a nonelectrical firing system 2-1
Figure 2-2. Components of the M18A1 claymore munition kit (with a nonelectrical firing system) 2-2
Figure 2-3. Shock tube assembly with pull initiator 2-3
Figure 2-4. M7 bandoleer 2-3
Figure 2-5. M7 bandoleer with sewn-in instructions 2-4
Figure 2-6. Inspecting an M7 bandoleer packed with an M18A1 claymore munition and a shock tube assembly with pull initiator 2-6

Figure 2-7. Positioning the M18A1 claymore munition with the front facing in the desired area of fire 2-7
Figure 2-8. Aiming an M18A1 claymore munition 2-8
Figure 2-9. Removing the nonelectrical blasting cap from the spool at the munition emplacement site 2-9
Figure 2-10. Unwinding approximately 1 meter (3 feet) of shock tube from the spool at the munition emplacement site 2-10
Figure 2-11. Securing the shock tube at the munition emplacement site 2-11
Figure 2-12. Arming an M18A1 claymore munition equipped with a nonelectrical firing system 2-12
Figure 2-13. Re-aiming an employed M18A1 claymore munition 2-12
Figure 2-14. Unwinding shock tube from the spool while moving back to the firing position 2-14
Figure 2-15. Securing shock tube at the firing position 2-15
Figure 2-16. Removing the igniter from the spool and pulling the igniter safety pin at the M18A1 claymore munition firing position 2-17
Figure 2-17. Firing an M18A1 claymore munition with an M81 initiator 2-17
Figure 2-18. Testing for powder in the shock tube 2-22
Figure 3-1. M18A1 claymore munition with an electrical firing system 3-1
Figure 3-2. Components of the M18A1 claymore munition kit (with an electrical firing system) 3-2
Figure 3-3. M57 firing device 3-3
Figure 3-4. M4 electrical blasting cap assembly 3-4
Figure 3-5. M40 test set 3-5
Figure 3-6. M7 bandoleer 3-6
Figure 3-7. M7 bandoleer with sewn-in instructions 3-6
Figure 3-8. Inspecting an M7 bandoleer packed with an M18A1 claymore munition and electrical firing system accessories 3-8
Figure 3-9. Plugging the M40 test set into the M57 firing device 3-9
Figure 3-10. Moving the M57 firing device from the SAFE position to the FIRE position 3-9
Figure 3-11. Conducting a circuit test of the M57 firing device while observing the window on the M40 test set 3-10
Figure 3-12. Unwinding approximately 1 meter (3 feet) of firing wire from spool at the firing position 3-12
Figure 3-13. Securing firing wire at the M18A1 claymore munition firing position 3-13
Figure 3-14. Placing the firing wire spool (with the blasting cap) under a sandbag 3-14
Figure 3-15. Plugging the firing wire connector into the M40 test set 3-14
Figure 3-16. Moving the M57 firing device from the SAFE position to the FIRE position 3-15
Figure 3-17. Conducting a circuit test of the firing wire while observing the window on the M40 test set 3-15
Figure 3-18. Unwinding firing wire from the spool while moving toward the munition emplacement site 3-17
Figure 3-19. Preparing the M18A1 claymore munition for emplacement 3-18

Figure 3-20. Positioning the M18A1 claymore munition with the front facing in the desired area of fire 3-19
Figure 3-21. Aiming an M18A1 claymore munition 3-20
Figure 3-22. Securing the firing wire at the munition emplacement site 3-21
Figure 3-23. Arming the M18A1 claymore munition equipped with an electrical firing system 3-22
Figure 3-24. Re-aiming an employed M18A1 claymore munition 3-22
Figure 3-25. Placing the firing wire spool with remainder of spooled wire in front of the M18A1 claymore munition 3-23
Figure 3-26. Firing an M18A1 claymore munition with an M57 firing device 3-26
Figure 5-1. Diagram of lateral separation pattern 5-2

Tables

Table 1-1. Technical specifications for the M18A1 claymore munition 1-2
Table 1-2. Firing systems and associated information 1-3
Table 3-1. Technical specifications for the M57 firing device 3-3
Table 3-2. Technical specifications for the M40 test set 3-5
Table 4-1. Task, conditions, and standards for employing the M18A1 claymore munition 4-9
Table 4-2. Task, conditions, and standards for disarming and recovering the M18A1 claymore munition 4-9
Table 5-1. Firing systems, methods of initiation, and their uses 5-1
Table 5-2. Uses for controlled dispersion 5-3
Table 5-3. Types of retrograde operations 5-4
Table 5-4. Types of offensive combat 5-5
Table 5-5. Types of ambush 5-8

Preface

Training Circular (TC) 3-22.23 provides technical information about training and employment of M18A1 claymore munitions. Intended users include leaders and Soldiers who use this information to successfully integrate M18A1 claymore munitions into their combat operations. The electrical system used to fire the M18A1 claymore munition has been replaced by a nonelectrical system, a shock tube assembly with pull initiator; however, M18A1 claymore munitions equipped with electrical firing systems will remain in the Army inventory until the current stock is exhausted.

This TC applies to the Active Army, the Army National Guard (ARNG)/Army National Guard of the United States (ARNGUS), and the United States Army Reserve (USAR) unless otherwise stated.

The proponent for this publication is the U.S. Army Training and Doctrine Command (TRADOC). The preparing agency is the Maneuver Center of Excellence (MCoE). You may send comments and recommendations by any means (U.S. mail, e-mail, fax, or telephone) as long as you use DA Form 2028 (*Recommended Changes to Publications and Blank Forms*) or follow its format. Point of contact information is as follows:

    E-mail: usarmy.benning.mcoe.mbx.229-s3-doc-lit@.mail.mil
    Phone: Commercial: 706-545-8623
              DSN: 835-8623
    Fax: Commercial: 706-545-8600
              DSN: 835-8600
    U.S. Mail: Commandant, MCoE
              ATTN: ATSH-INB
              6850 Barron Avenue, Bldg 85
              Fort Benning, GA 31905-5593

Unless this publication states otherwise, masculine nouns and pronouns do not refer exclusively to men.

This page intentionally left blank.

Chapter 1
Description, Capabilities, and Components

The M18A1 claymore munition (Figure 1-1) is a directional, fixed-fragmentation munition. It is primarily designed for use against massed Infantry attacks; however, its fragments are also effective against light-armored vehicles.

Figure 1-1. M18A1 claymore munition

EFFECTS

1-1. When detonated at a range of 50 meters, the M18A1 claymore munition delivers spherical steel fragments over a 60-degree, fan-shaped pattern that is 2 meters high and 50 meters wide. These fragments are moderately effective up to a range of 100 meters and can travel up to 250 meters forward of the munition. The optimal effective range (the range at which the most desirable balance is achieved between lethality and area coverage) is 50 meters.

COMPONENTS

1-2. The munition and its accessories are carried in a bandoleer. The accessories vary according to the type of firing system used.

> *Note.* Chapters 2 and 3 provide more information about the bandoleer and other accessories.

MUNITION

1-3. Table 1-1 lists the technical specifications for the munition.

Note. The M18A1 claymore munition can function for 2 hours after it has been submerged in salt or fresh water.

Table 1-1. Technical specifications for the M18A1 claymore munition

NOMENCLATURE	Munition, directional fragmentation, M18A1
COMMON NAME	Claymore
TYPE	Antipersonnel
WEIGHT	3 1/2 pounds
LENGTH	8 1/2 inches
WIDTH	1 3/8 inches
HEIGHT	5 1/2 inches (legs folded)
FIRING UNIT CONSTRUCTION	The outer surface of the munition is a curved, rectangular, olive drab, molded case of fiberglass-filled polystyrene (plastic). In the front portion of the case is a fragmentation face containing steel spheres embedded in a plastic matrix. The back portion of the case (behind the matrix) contains a layer of explosive material.
EXPLOSIVE	1 1/2 pounds of composition C4
DETONATOR WELLS	The two detonator wells, located on the top of the munition allow for single or dual priming. These wells are sealed by the plug ends of the shipping plug priming adapters to prevent foreign materials from entering the detonator wells. The slotted end of the shipping plug priming adapter is used to hold an electrical blasting cap in place when the munition is armed. The shipping plug priming adapter is merely reversed when the munition is to be armed. *Note.* J007 will accept both nonelectric and electric blasting caps. K143 and K145 will only accept electric blasting caps.
SIGHT AND ARROWS	The sight and arrows located on top of the munition are used to aim the munition. The M18A1 claymore munition is equipped with a fixed plastic knife-edge sight or slit-type peepsight on earlier models.
LEGS	Two pairs of folding legs, located on the bottom of the munition enable it to be emplaced on the ground. The munition can also be tied to posts, trees, and other things.

FIRING SYSTEMS

1-4. Operators can initiate M18A1 claymore munitions using nonelectrical and electrical firing systems. Table 1-2 provides more information about these firing systems.

Description, Capabilities, and Components

Table 1-2. Firing systems and associated information

FIRING SYSTEM	METHODS OF INITIATION
Nonelectrical	Shock tube assembly with pull initiator
	Time fuze attached to detonating cord with pull initiator
	Note. This is used as an alternative method of initiation and can be used for dual priming.
Electrical	M4 blasting cap with M57 firing device

Nonelectrical Firing Systems

1-5. Nonelectrical firing systems use heat and pressure to detonate the munition. When using this firing system, an operator can use two methods to initiate detonation:
- Shock tube assembly with pull initiator.
- Time fuze attached to detonating cord with pull initiator.

Note. In newer versions of the M18A1 claymore munition, the nonelectrical system, a shock tube assembly with pull initiator, has replaced the electrical system used to fire the M18A1 claymore munition; however, the electrical system is still in use. The nonelectrical system provides an easier, safer, and more reliable means of initiation. This modification resulted in a 3-pound weight savings for the operator.

Electrical Firing Systems

1-6. When equipped with a firing wire assembly, the M18A1 claymore munition uses electricity generated by the M57 firing device to detonate the M4 blasting cap and the munition.

Note. One M57 electrical firing device is issued with each M18A1 claymore munition.

SAFETY

1-7. Operators must consider the safety of friendly troops when employing M18A1 claymore munitions.

DANGER FROM FRAGMENTS

1-8. The danger area consists of a 180-degree fan with a radius of 250 meters centered in the direction of aim (Figure 1-2).

DANGER AREA OF BACKBLAST AND SECONDARY MISSILES

> **DANGER**
>
> FRIENDLY TROOPS ARE PROHIBITED IN AREAS TO THE REAR AND SIDES OF THE MUNITION WITHIN A RADIUS OF 16 METERS.
>
> THE MINIMUM SAFE OPERATING DISTANCE FROM THE MUNITION IS 16 METERS. AT THIS DISTANCE, THE OPERATOR MUST BE POSITIONED IN A FOXHOLE, BEHIND COVER, OR LYING PRONE IN A DEPRESSION.
>
> THE OPERATOR AND ALL FRIENDLY TROOPS WITHIN 100 METERS OF THE MUNITION MUST TAKE COVER TO PREVENT BEING INJURED BY FLYING SECONDARY OBJECTS (SUCH AS STICKS, STONES, AND PEBBLES).

Chapter 1

> **WARNING**
>
> Before detonating an M18A1 claymore munition, operators must use appropriate hearing protection. Single hearing protection is required for all personnel within 90 meters (300 feet) of the munition.

1-9. The operator and all friendly troops within an area of 16 meters to the rear and sides of the munition's backblast must take cover to prevent ruptured eardrums or injury from secondary missile hazards (Figure 1-2).

1-10. When firing a munition attached to a tree or other object, operators must take care to avoid secondary missile hazards. Before firing the munition, friendly troops in a 16- to 100-meter radius in a 180-degree arc must be in a covered position.

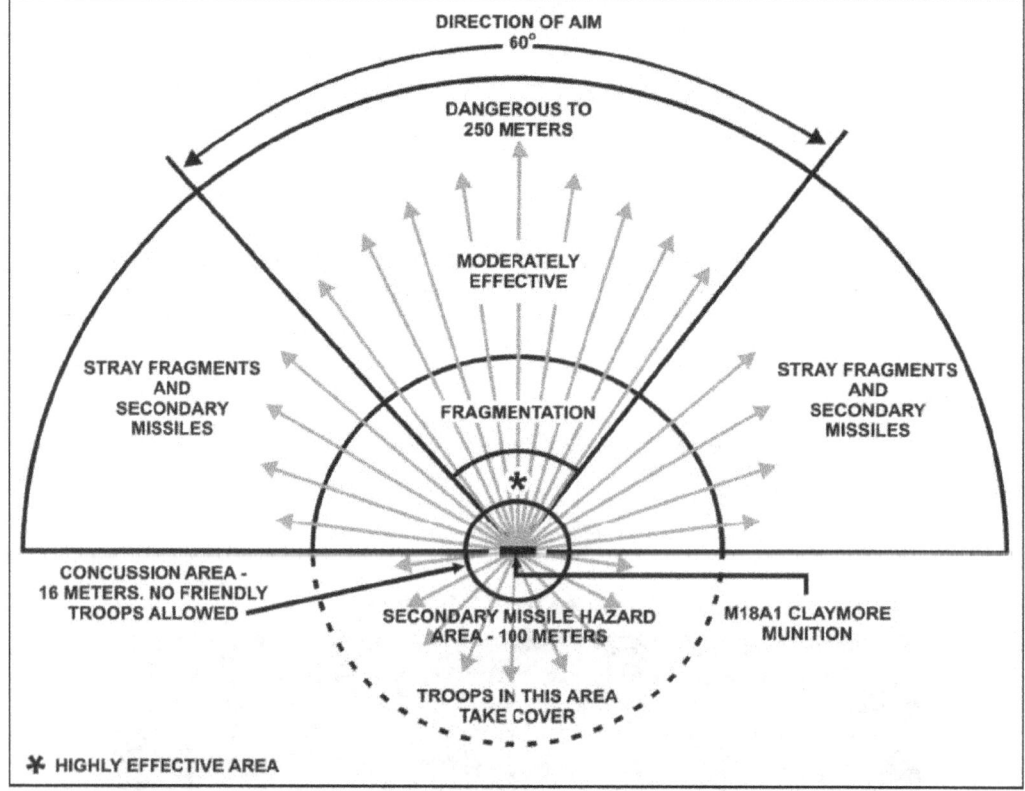

Figure 1-2. Danger radius and effects of the M18A1 claymore munition

Chapter 2
Method of Initiation: Shock Tube Assembly With Pull Initiator

The nonelectrical system, a shock tube assembly with pull initiator, has replaced the electrical system used to fire the M18A1 claymore munition (Figure 2-1). The nonelectrical system provides an easier, safer, and more reliable means of initiation.

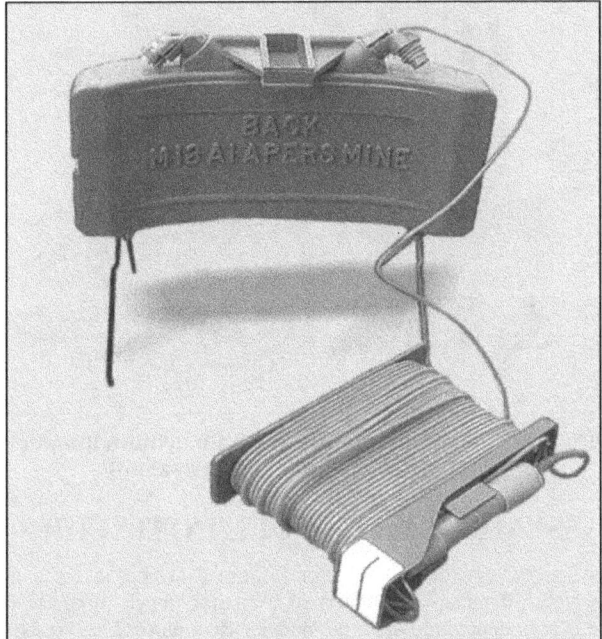

Figure 2-1. M18A1 claymore munition with a nonelectrical firing system

SECTION I. COMPONENTS

2-1. In addition to the M18A1 claymore munition, the kit comes with the following accessories (Figure 2-2):
- Shock tube assembly with pull initiator.
- M7 bandoleer.

Chapter 2

Figure 2-2. Components of the M18A1 claymore munition kit
(with a nonelectrical firing system)

SHOCK TUBE ASSEMBLY WITH PULL INITIATOR

2-2. The shock tube assembly with pull initiator (Figure 2-3) consists of a nonelectrical blasting cap attached to approximately 30 meters (100 feet) of miniature shock tube. On one side of the spool of miniature shock tube is an indentation where the nonelectrical blasting cap rests; this protects the blasting cap. Attached to the opposite end of the shock tube is an M81 igniter. A barrier bag protects this firing assembly from the elements.

2-3. When using a shock tube assembly with pull initiator, setup and firing time are reduced. Because the shock tube assembly with pull initiator is a nonelectrical component, there is no electrical wire to test. There is no need to cut away any excess tube, since the shock tube's ends are factory-sealed to make it moisture-proof. The igniter is preinstalled; as soon as the operator removes the munition from its packaging, the munition is ready to fire.

Method of Initiation: Shock Tube Assembly With Pull Initiator

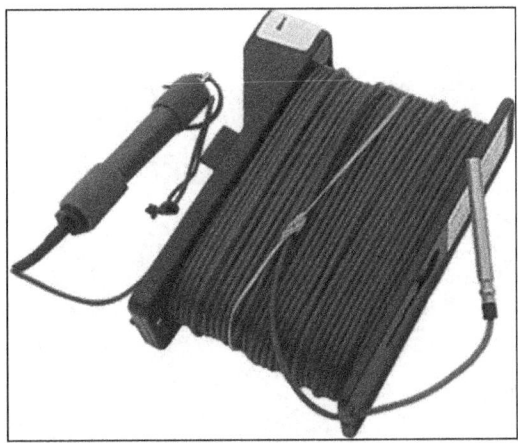

Figure 2-3. Shock tube assembly with pull initiator

M7 BANDOLEER

2-4. The operator carries the munition and its accessories in an M7 bandoleer (Figure 2-4). The M7 bandoleer is constructed of olive drab, water-resistant canvas and has snap fasteners to secure the flap. The bandoleer has two pockets: one pocket contains the munition, and the other contains a shock tube assembly with pull initiator. A 2-inch wide, webbed shoulder carrying strap is sewn to the bag. An instruction sheet for operation is sewn to the inside flap of the M7 bandoleer (Figure 2-5).

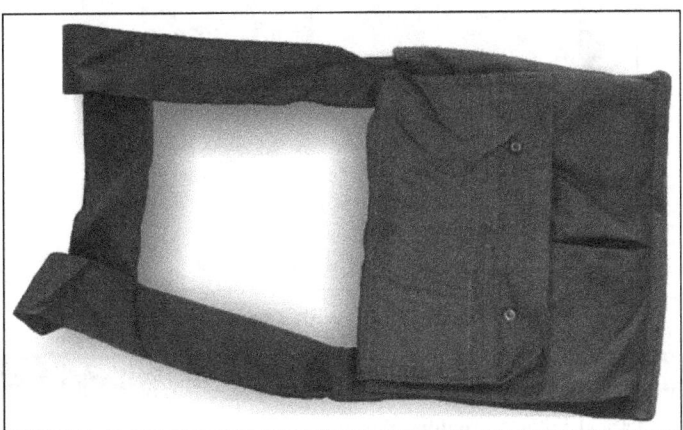

Figure 2-4. M7 bandoleer

Chapter 2

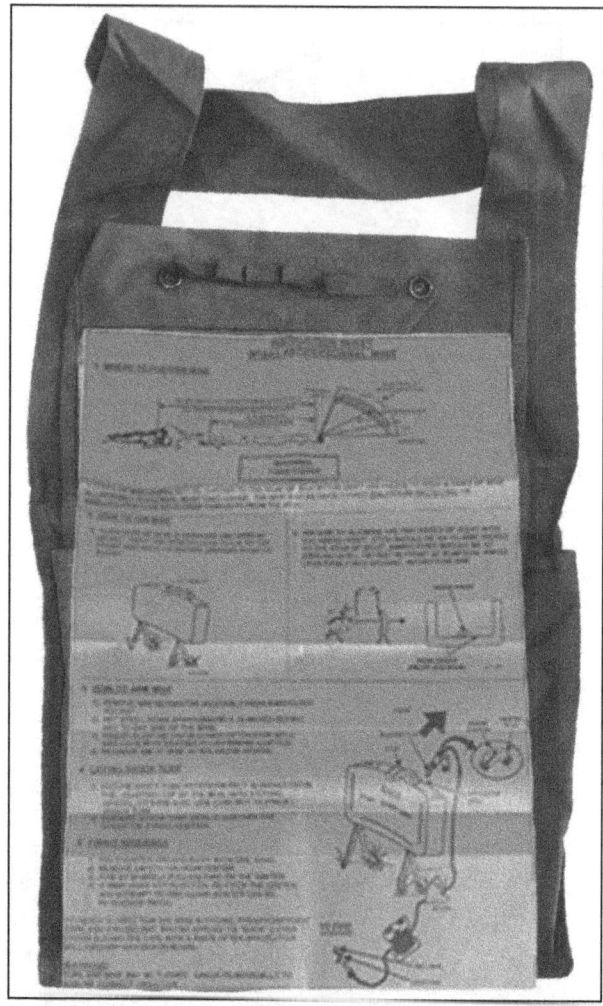

Figure 2-5. M7 bandoleer with sewn-in instructions

SECTION II. STANDARD OPERATION

2-5. During nonelectrical initiation, pulling the ring on the M81 igniter detonates the blasting cap. The detonation of the blasting cap, in turn, sets off a high-explosive charge.

Note. All operators should read the instruction sheet inside of the bandoleer cover before employing the munition.

Method of Initiation: Shock Tube Assembly With Pull Initiator

> **DANGER**
> ALL OPERATORS MUST WEAR LEATHER-PALMED GLOVES WHEN HANDLING BLASTING CAPS. OPERATORS MUST NOT TOUCH THE BLASTING CAP WITH THEIR BARE HANDS. THIS CAN CAUSE UNINTENTIONAL DETONATION OF THE BLASTING CAP.

2-6. With an understanding of how to employ the munition, the operator—
- Selects and prepares a firing position.
- Employs the munition.
- Aims the munition.
- Arms the munition.
- Camouflages the munition.
- Fires the munition.

SELECTING AND PREPARING A FIRING POSITION

> **DANGER**
> FRIENDLY TROOPS ARE PROHIBITED IN AREAS TO THE REAR AND SIDES OF THE MUNITION WITHIN A RADIUS OF 16 METERS.
>
> THE MINIMUM SAFE OPERATING DISTANCE FROM THE MUNITION IS 16 METERS. AT THIS DISTANCE, THE OPERATOR MUST BE POSITIONED IN A FOXHOLE, BEHIND COVER, OR LYING PRONE IN A DEPRESSION.
>
> THE OPERATOR AND ALL FRIENDLY TROOPS WITHIN 100 METERS OF THE MUNITION MUST TAKE COVER TO PREVENT BEING INJURED BY FLYING SECONDARY OBJECTS (SUCH AS STICKS, STONES, AND PEBBLES).

2-7. The operator should select a firing position that offers cover and unobstructed observation of the site selected for emplacing the munition.

2-8. Once the operator has selected and prepared a firing position, he performs the following procedures:
   (1) Place the bandoleer on the shoulder or around the neck.
   (2) Ensure that the munition and all accessories are in the bandoleer (Figure 2-6).
   (3) Move to the site selected for emplacing the munition.

Note. Chapter 5 provides more information about selecting a site for munition emplacement.

Chapter 2

Figure 2-6. Inspecting an M7 bandoleer packed with an M18A1 claymore munition and a shock tube assembly with pull initiator

EMPLOYING

2-9. To employ the munition, the operator performs the following procedures:

> **DANGER**
>
> SINCE THE IGNITER IS PERMANENTLY ATTACHED TO THE SHOCK TUBE, THE OPERATOR MUST UNCOIL THE TUBE FROM THE MUNITION EMPLACEMENT SITE TO THE FIRING POSITION.
>
> THE SHOCK TUBE ASSEMBLY WITH PULL INITIATOR CONTAINS APPROXIMATELY 30 METERS (100 FEET) OF MINIATURE SHOCK TUBE. WHEN SELECTING MUNITION EMPLACEMENT SITES, THE OPERATOR MUST ENSURE THAT PROTECTIVE COVER IS LOCATED WITHIN THIS RANGE.
>
> THE OPERATOR MUST POSITION THE M18A1 CLAYMORE MUNITION SO THAT FRIENDLY PERSONNEL TO THE REAR AND SIDES OF THE MUNITION WILL NOT BE ENDANGERED. THE FIRING POSITION MUST BE AT LEAST 16 METERS TO THE REAR OR SIDES OF THE MUNITION.

(1) Remove the munition from the bandoleer.

Method of Initiation: Shock Tube Assembly With Pull Initiator

(2) Turn the legs rearward and then downward.
(3) Spread each pair of legs approximately 45 degrees.

Note. One leg should protrude to the front of the munition, and one to the rear of the munition (Figure 2-7).

> **DANGER**
> THE OPERATOR MUST ENSURE THAT THE MUNITION IS POSITIONED WITH THE SURFACE MARKED "FRONT TOWARD ENEMY" AND THE ARROWS ON TOP OF THE MUNITION POINTING IN THE DIRECTION OF THE ENEMY OR THE DESIRED AREA OF FIRE.

(4) Position the munition with the surface marked "FRONT TOWARD ENEMY" and the arrows on top of the munition pointing in the direction of the enemy or the desired area of fire (Figure 2-7).
(5) Press the legs approximately 1/3 of the way into the ground.

Note. To prevent tipping in windy areas or when the legs cannot be pressed into the ground, the operator spreads the legs to the maximum breadth (approximately 180 degrees, so that the legs are to the front and rear of the munition). On snow or extremely soft ground, the bandoleer may be spread beneath the munition for support.

(6) Aim the munition.

Figure 2-7. Positioning the M18A1 claymore munition with the front facing in the desired area of fire

AIMING

2-10. To aim the munition (Figure 2-8), the operator performs the following procedures:
  (1) Select an aiming point that is at ground level and approximately 50 meters (150 feet) in front of the munition.
  (2) Position the eye approximately 6 inches (15 centimeters) to the rear of the sight.
  (3) Aim the munition by aligning the two edges of the sight with the aiming point.

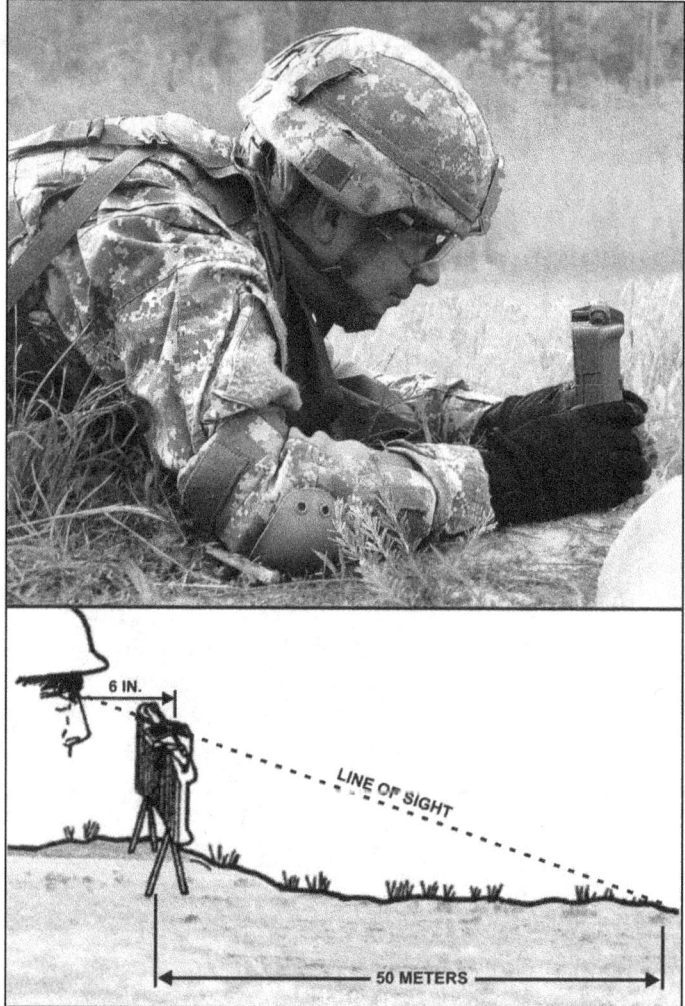

Figure 2-8. Aiming an M18A1 claymore munition

Method of Initiation: Shock Tube Assembly With Pull Initiator

ARMING

> **WARNING**
>
> Operators must not yank or pull on the shock tube, blasting cap, or igniter. The shock tube, blasting cap, and igniter are factory-sealed. Stretching or yanking on the nonelectrical firing system may cause separation, creating a system misfire.
>
> After handling the shock tube, operators must wash their hands before eating or drinking.

2-11. To arm the munition, the operator performs the following procedures:
    (1) Remove the rubber band that secures the blasting cap to the spool.
    (2) Remove the blasting cap from the spool's cavity (Figure 2-9).

> **DANGER**
> ALL OPERATORS MUST WEAR LEATHER-PALMED GLOVES WHEN HANDLING BLASTING CAPS. OPERATORS MUST NOT TOUCH THE BLASTING CAP WITH THEIR BARE HANDS. THIS CAN CAUSE UNINTENTIONAL DETONATION OF THE BLASTING CAP.

Figure 2-9. Removing the nonelectrical blasting cap from the spool at the munition emplacement site

(3) Unwind approximately 1 meter (3 feet) of shock tube. To measure 1 meter of shock tube (Figure 2-10)—

> *Notes.* 1. As the operator uncoils the shock tube, he should ensure that it does not become tangled or kinked.
>
> 2. The distance from the center of the operator's chest to one arm's length is approximately 1 meter (3 feet).

- Hold the blasting cap against the center of the chest with the left hand.
- Encircle the shock tube at the base of the blasting cap with the index finger and thumb of the right hand.
- While holding the right hand to the chest, extend the left hand to arm's length, allowing the shock tube to be pulled through the fingers of the right hand.
- Lock the elbow, and pull all slack from the shock tube.

Figure 2-10. Unwinding approximately 1 meter (3 feet) of shock tube from the spool at the munition emplacement site

(4) At the 1-meter mark, fold the shock tube to create a loop with a large enough circumference to go around the chosen stake (Figure 2-11, A).

(5) Twist the loop over the index and middle fingers of the right hand (Figure 2-11, B).

(6) Push the loop through the circle created during Step (5) (Figure 2-11, C).

(7) Secure the shock tube from the blasting cap side of the munition to a stake (Figure 2-11, D) or a fixed object at the munition emplacement site. This prevents the munition from being misaligned if the shock tube is disturbed.

Method of Initiation: Shock Tube Assembly With Pull Initiator

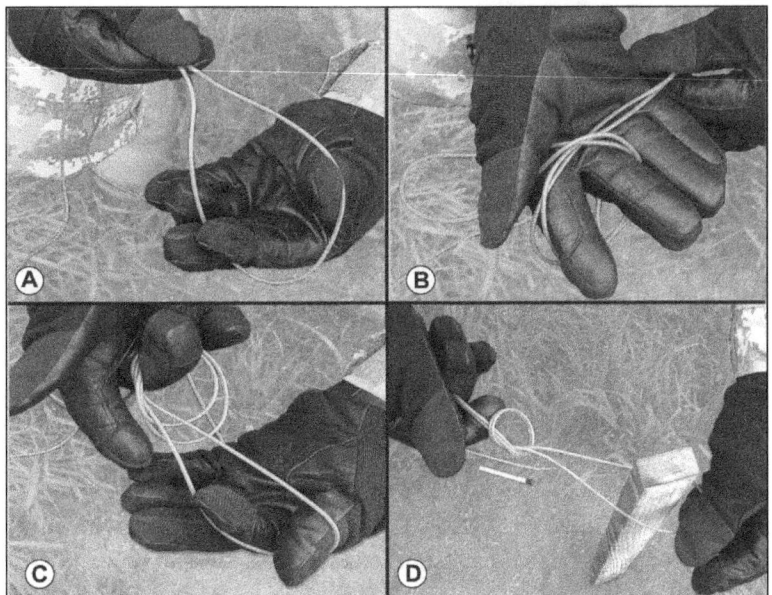

Figure 2-11. Securing the shock tube at the munition emplacement site

(8) Unscrew counterclockwise and invert the shipping plug priming adapter nearest to the stake or anchor (Figure 2-12, A).

(9) Slide the slotted end of the shipping plug priming adapter onto the shock tube between the crimped connections and the blasting cap (Figure 2-12, B).

(10) Pull the shock tube through the shipping plug priming adapter until the top of the blasting cap is firmly seated in the bottom portion of the shipping plug priming adapter (Figure 2-12, C).

(11) Insert the blasting cap, and screw the adapter clockwise into the detonator well (Figure 2-12, D).

(12) Re-aim the munition to ensure that the point of aim has not changed (Figure 2-13).

Chapter 2

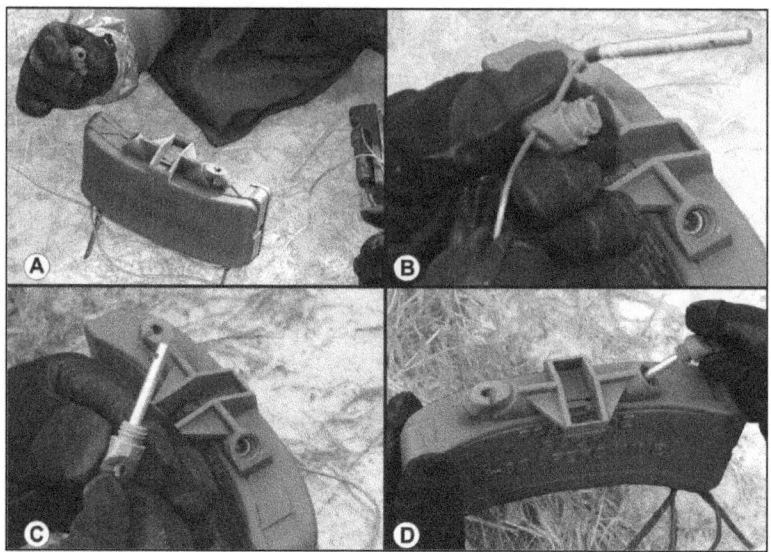

Figure 2-12. Arming an M18A1 claymore munition equipped with a nonelectrical firing system

Figure 2-13. Re-aiming an employed M18A1 claymore munition

Method of Initiation: Shock Tube Assembly With Pull Initiator

> **DANGER**
>
> SINCE THE IGNITER IS PERMANENTLY ATTACHED TO THE SHOCK TUBE, THE OPERATOR MUST UNCOIL THE TUBE FROM THE MUNITION EMPLACEMENT SITE TO THE FIRING POSITION.
>
> THE SHOCK TUBE ASSEMBLY WITH PULL INITIATOR CONTAINS APPROXIMATELY 30 METERS (100 FEET) OF MINIATURE SHOCK TUBE. WHEN SELECTING MUNITION EMPLACEMENT SITES, THE OPERATOR MUST ENSURE THAT PROTECTIVE COVER IS LOCATED WITHIN THIS RANGE.

Note. The operator should camouflage the munition before leaving the emplacement site, and camouflage the shock tube as he returns to his firing position. The following section provides more information about camouflage.

(13) Unwind the remaining shock tube as he returns to the firing position (Figure 2-14).

Note. As the operator uncoils the shock tube, he should make sure that it does not become tangled or kinked.

Figure 2-14. Unwinding shock tube from the spool while moving back to the firing position

(14) Secure the shock tube to a stake or a fixed object at the firing position (Figure 2-15). This prevents the munition from being misaligned if the shock tube is disturbed.

Note. The operator should follow the same procedures used to secure the shock tube at the munition emplacement site.

Figure 2-15. Securing shock tube at the firing position

CAMOUFLAGING

> **WARNING**
>
> When camouflaging the munition, the operator must use only lightweight foliage, such as leaves and grass, to avoid increasing the secondary missile hazard to the rear of the munition.
>
> After handling the shock tube, operators must wash their hands before eating or drinking.

2-12. Although the M18A1 claymore munition is painted olive drab to facilitate camouflaging, the operator should blend it into its surroundings to prevent its detection. When doing so, he should camouflage both the front and rear of the munition with foliage. He should also camouflage the shock tube or bury it underground.

Note. TC 3-21.75 provides more information about the principles and methods of camouflage.

Chapter 2

FIRING

> **WARNING**
>
> Before detonating an M18A1 claymore munition, operators must use appropriate hearing protection. Single hearing protection is required for all personnel within 90 meters (300 feet) of the munition.
>
> The operator must not remove the safety pin (cotter pin) until the actual time of firing.
>
> After handling the shock tube, operators must wash their hands before eating or drinking.

> **DANGER**
>
> BEFORE REMOVING THE SAFETY PIN (COTTER PIN), THE OPERATOR MUST ENSURE THAT ALL FRIENDLY TROOPS WITHIN 250 METERS OF THE FRONT AND SIDES AND 100 METERS OF THE REAR OF THE MUNITION ARE UNDER COVER.

2-13. To fire the munition, the operator performs the following procedures:
   (1) Seek cover.
   (2) Remove the igniter from the spool (Figure 2-16, A).
   (3) Remove the safety pin (cotter pin) on the igniter (Figure 2-16, B), and place it in the bandoleer for possible use later.

Note. Tactical situations may dictate the performance of Step (4).

   (4) Alert friendly personnel by announcing "CLAYMORE" twice (depending on the situation).

Method of Initiation: Shock Tube Assembly With Pull Initiator

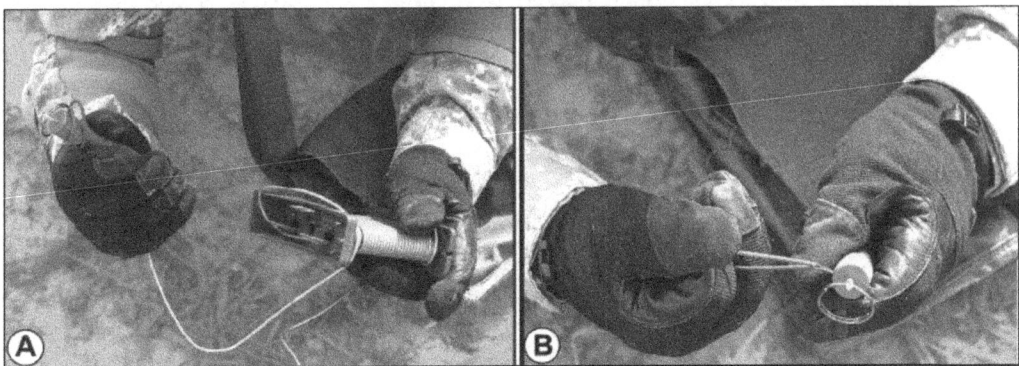

Figure 2-16. Removing the igniter from the spool and pulling the igniter safety pin at the M18A1 claymore munition firing position

WARNING

Operators must not hold the shock tube while firing. This can cause minor burns as the flame burns through the tube.

The igniter forward end opening (shock tube insertion point) can emit hot, gaseous byproducts when the munition is initiated. When firing the igniter, the operator must keep his hands clear of this area.

After handling the shock tube, operators must wash their hands before eating or drinking.

The operator must wear leather-palmed gloves when firing the igniter.

(5) While holding the body of the igniter with one hand, insert the index finger of the other hand into the pull ring (Figure 2-17, A).
(6) While holding the body of the igniter, turn the pull ring ¼ to the right or left. Then, pull the ring sharply (Figure 2-17, B).

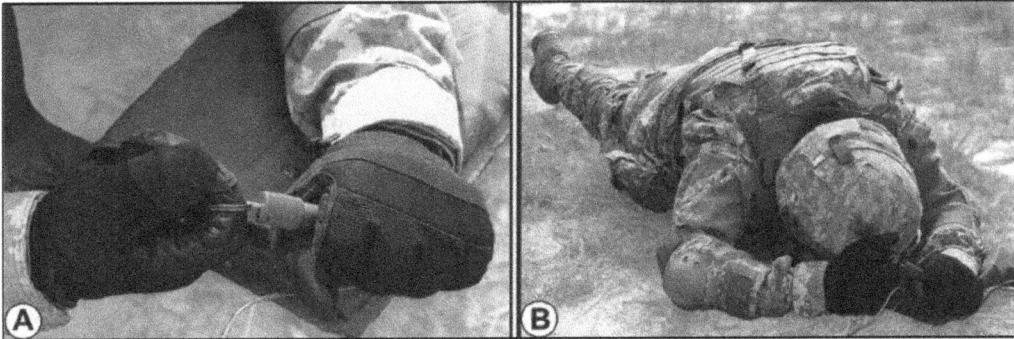

Figure 2-17. Firing an M18A1 claymore munition with an M81 initiator

Chapter 2

SECTION III. OPERATION UNDER UNUSUAL CONDITIONS

2-14. Operators must be capable of employing M18A1 claymore munitions under various operational conditions. Operators may also encounter events that change normal operation of the munition, such as misfires. Other situations may require disarming, recovering, or destroying the munition.

ADDRESSING A MISFIRE

2-15. A misfire is a complete failure to fire caused by a procedural or mechanical failure.

Note. Operators should notify a supervisor and ammunition supply point (ASP) of any unusual occurrence, regardless of whether the munition fires or not.

2-16. The procedures vary according to the type of mission: operational or training.

Note. TM 9-1345-203-12 provides more information about proper misfire procedures.

OPERATIONAL MISSION

2-17. If the munition fails to function after the operator has pulled the igniter, he should perform the following procedures:

> **WARNING**
>
> After handling the shock tube, operators must wash their hands before eating or drinking.

(1) If the munition is dual-primed, attempt to fire using the secondary initiation device. If the munition still fails to fire, continue using the following procedures.

(2) Recock the igniter. While holding the body of the igniter, turn the pull ring ¼ to the right or left, and push it all of the way in.

Note. The igniter can be recocked twice.

> **WARNING**
>
> The operator must wear leather-palmed gloves when firing the igniter.
>
> Operators must not hold the shock tube while firing. This can cause minor burns as the flame burns through the tube.
>
> The igniter forward end opening (shock tube insertion point) can emit hot, gaseous byproducts when the munition is initiated. When firing the igniter, the operator must keep his hands clear of this area.

(3) Attempt to fire again.

Method of Initiation: Shock Tube Assembly With Pull Initiator

Note. Tactical situations may dictate the performance of Step (4).

(4) If the igniter fails to fire again, announce "MISFIRE" three times (depending on the situation).
(5) When time and circumstances allow, locate an M81 igniter.
(6) If an M81 igniter is not available or time and circumstances do not permit, the munition is now to be treated as unexploded ordnance. If this occurs, notify your supervisor, refer to unit SOP, and notify higher headquarters. EOD must be notified for proper disposal of a misfire.

> **DANGER**
>
> IF THE MUNITION FAILS TO INITIATE, EOD PERSONNEL MUST WAIT 30 MINUTES BEFORE APPROACHING THE MUNITION. NO OTHER PERSONNEL SHOULD APPROACH THE MUNITION.

Alternate Step (6). If an additional M81 igniter is available, an NCOIC should supervise the following steps. Remove the original igniter. To do so—

- Measure approximately 1 meter (roughly 3 feet) of shock tube from the place where the igniter is installed.

> **WARNING**
>
> After handling the shock tube, operators must wash their hands before eating or drinking.
>
> Operators must not ingest or inhale the explosive powder in the shock tube. The operator must not place the shock tube into his mouth or to his lips. Instead, he must keep the shock tube at least 1 to 2 inches from the mouth or lips. Failure to heed this warning can result in mild to moderate skin irritation.

- Cut the shock tube at that point with a knife, making a straight 90-degree cut and being careful not to crimp the shock tube.

(7) Install the new igniter.

> **WARNING**
>
> The operator must wear leather-palmed gloves when firing the igniter.
>
> Operators must not hold the shock tube while firing. This can cause minor burns as the flame burns through the tube.
>
> The igniter forward end opening (shock tube insertion point) can emit hot, gaseous byproducts when the munition is initiated. When firing the igniter, the operator must keep his hands clear of this area.

(8) Attempt to fire again.

Note. Tactical situations may dictate the performance of Step (9).

(9) If the igniter fails to fire again, announce "MISFIRE" three times (depending on the situation).
(10) If an additional M81 igniter is not available or time and circumstances do not permit, the munition is now to be treated as unexploded ordnance. If this occurs, notify his supervisor, refer to unit SOP, and notify higher headquarters. EOD must be notified for proper disposal of a misfire.

> **DANGER**
>
> IF THE MUNITION FAILS TO INITIATE, EOD PERSONNEL MUST WAIT 30 MINUTES BEFORE APPROACHING THE MUNITION. NO OTHER PERSONNEL SHOULD APPROACH THE MUNITION.

TRAINING

2-18. If the munition fails to function after the operator has pulled the igniter, he should perform the following procedures:
(1) If the munition is dual-primed, attempt to fire using the secondary initiation device. If the munition still fails to fire, continue using the following procedures.
(2) Announce 'MISFIRE" three times.
(3) Recock the igniter. While holding the body of the igniter, turn the pull ring ¼ to the right or left, and push it all of the way in.

Note. The igniter can be recocked twice.

> **WARNING**
>
> The operator must wear leather-palmed gloves when firing the igniter.
>
> Operators must not hold the shock tube while firing. This can cause minor burns as the flame burns through the tube.
>
> The igniter forward end opening (shock tube insertion point) can emit hot, gaseous byproducts when the munition is initiated. When firing the igniter, the operator must keep his hands clear of this area.

(4) Attempt to fire again.
(5) If the igniter fails to fire again, announce "MISFIRE" three times.
(6) Consider the three possible courses of action based on the following conditions:
- Additional M81 igniter is available.
- Additional M81 igniter is not available, but additional shock tube assembly with pull initiator is available.
- Neither an additional M81 igniter nor an additional shock tube assembly with pull initiator is available.

Additional M81 Igniter is Available

2-19. To perform this method, the operator performs the following procedures:

Note. The following steps must be supervised by equipment-certified range cadre. TM 9-1345-203-12 outlines additional guidance regarding proper misfire procedures.

Method of Initiation: Shock Tube Assembly With Pull Initiator

(1) Request an M81 igniter.
(2) Remove the original igniter. To do so—
- Measure approximately 1 meter (roughly 3 feet) of shock tube from the place where the igniter is installed.

> **WARNING**
>
> After handling the shock tube, operators must wash their hands before eating or drinking.
>
> Operators must not ingest or inhale the explosive powder in the shock tube. The operator must not place the shock tube into his mouth or to his lips. Instead, he must keep the shock tube at least 1 to 2 inches from the mouth or lips. Failure to heed this warning can result in mild to moderate skin irritation.

- Cut the shock tube at that point with a knife, making a straight 90-degree cut and being careful not to crimp the shock tube.

(3) Cut an additional 6 inches of shock tube off.

> **WARNING**
>
> The operator must not place the shock tube into his mouth or to his lips. Instead, he must keep the shock tube at least 1 to 2 inches from the mouth or lips. Failure to heed this warning can result in mild to moderate skin irritation.

(4) Conduct the blow test (Figure 2-18). To conduct the blow test, place one end of the 6-inch piece of shock tube in the palm of the hand, and place the other end at least 1 or 2 inches from the mouth. Blow through the tube.
- If a small amount of silver-colored powder is present, install a new igniter, and attempt to fire.
- If no silver-colored powder is present, measure an additional meter (3 feet) of shock tube, make a cut, and conduct another blow test on that piece of shock tube. Repeat two additional times (up to 3 meters [9 feet]) or until silver powder appears in the palm of the hand.

Chapter 2

Figure 2-18. Testing for powder in the shock tube

(5) Install a new igniter.

> **WARNING**
>
> The operator must wear leather-palmed gloves when firing the igniter.
>
> Operators must not hold the shock tube while firing. This can cause minor burns as the flame burns through the tube.
>
> The igniter forward end opening (shock tube insertion point) can emit hot, gaseous byproducts when the munition is initiated. When firing the igniter, the operator must keep his hands clear of this area.

(6) Attempt to fire again.
(7) If the igniter fails to fire again, announce "MISFIRE" three times.
(8) If the blasting cap assembly activates but the munition fails to function, the munition is now to be treated as unexploded ordnance. If this occurs, notify an immediate supervisor, refer to unit SOP for procedures regarding misfire reporting (if the tactical situation permits), and notify higher headquarters. EOD must be notified for proper disposal of a misfire.

> **DANGER**
> IF THE MUNITION FAILS TO INITIATE, EOD PERSONNEL MUST WAIT 30 MINUTES BEFORE APPROACHING THE MUNITION. NO OTHER PERSONNEL SHOULD APPROACH THE MUNITION.

Method of Initiation: Shock Tube Assembly With Pull Initiator

Additional M81 Igniter is not Available, but Additional Shock Tube Assembly With Pull Initiator is Available

2-20. If an M81 igniter is not available but an additional shock tube assembly with pull initiator is available—

(1) Notify a supervisor and range cadre.

Note. The following steps must be supervised by equipment-certified range cadre. TM 9-1345-203-12 provides more information about proper misfire procedures.

(2) Remove the original igniter. To do so—
- Measure approximately 1 meter (roughly 3 feet) of shock tube from the place where the igniter is installed.

> **WARNING**
>
> After handling the shock tube, operators must wash their hands before eating or drinking.
>
> Operators must not ingest or inhale the explosive powder in the shock tube. The operator must not place the shock tube into his mouth or to his lips. Instead, he must keep the shock tube at least 1 to 2 inches from the mouth or lips. Failure to heed this warning can result in mild to moderate skin irritation.

- Cut the shock tube at that point with a knife, making a straight 90-degree cut and being careful not to crimp the shock tube.

(3) Cut an additional 6 inches of shock tube off.

(4) Conduct the blow test. To conduct the blow test, blow through those 6 inches with the open end of the shock tube in the palm of the hand.

> **WARNING**
>
> After handling the shock tube, operators must wash their hands before eating or drinking.
>
> Operators must not ingest or inhale the explosive powder in the shock tube. The operator must not place the shock tube into his mouth or to his lips. Instead, he must keep the shock tube at least 1 to 2 inches from the mouth or lips. Failure to heed this warning can result in mild to moderate skin irritation.

- If a small amount of silver-colored powder is present, install a new igniter, and attempt to fire.
- If no silver-colored powder is present, measure an additional meter (3 feet) of shock tube, make a cut, and conduct another blow test on that piece of shock tube. Repeat two additional times (up to 3 meters [9 feet]) or until silver-colored powder appears in the palm of the hand.

(5) Approximately 3 inches from the cut end, fold the shock tube onto itself, creating a groove.

(6) Place the blasting cap of the second shock tube assembly into the groove created by folding the shock tube.

(7) Using duct or electrical tape, tape the blasting cap securely in the groove. Tape the area fully.

> **DANGER**
>
> UPON DETONATION, BLASTING CAPS PRODUCE SMALL PROJECTILES THAT CAN INJURE PERSONNEL. THE OPERATOR MUST PLACE THE TAPED BLASTING CAP/SHOCK TUBE IN A SAFE LOCATION FORWARD OF HIS COVERED POSITION, SUCH AS UNDER A SANDBAG OR ON THE OPPOSITE SIDE OF THE WALL OR BERM THAT PROVIDES COVER FOR THE OPERATOR. HOWEVER, HE MUST NOT APPROACH THE MUNITION.

(8) Place the taped blasting cap/shock tube in a safe location forward of the covered position, such as under a sandbag or on the opposite side of the wall or berm that provides cover for the operator. However, DO NOT APPROACH THE MUNITION.

(9) Unwind the appropriate amount of shock tube from the new shock tube assembly as you return to the firing position.

Note. As the operator uncoils the shock tube, he must ensure that it does not become tangled or kinked.

> **WARNING**
>
> The operator must wear leather-palmed gloves when firing the igniter.
>
> Operators must not hold the shock tube while firing. This can cause minor burns as the flame burns through the tube.
>
> The igniter forward end opening (shock tube insertion point) can emit hot, gaseous byproducts when the munition is initiated. When firing the igniter, the operator must keep his hands clear of this area.

(10) Attempt to fire using the igniter of the new shock tube assembly.
(11) If the igniter fails to fire again, announce "MISFIRE" three times.
(12) Recock the igniter. While holding the body of the igniter, turn the pull ring ¼ to the right or left, and push it all of the way in.

Note. The igniter can be recocked twice.

Method of Initiation: Shock Tube Assembly With Pull Initiator

> **WARNING**
>
> The operator must wear leather-palmed gloves when firing the igniter.
>
> Operators must not hold the shock tube while firing. This can cause minor burns as the flame burns through the tube.
>
> The igniter forward end opening (shock tube insertion point) can emit hot, gaseous byproducts when the munition is initiated. When firing the igniter, the operator must keep his hands clear of this area.

(13) Attempt to fire again.
(14) If the igniter fails to fire again, announce "MISFIRE" three times.
(15) If the blasting cap assembly activates but the munition fails to function, the munition is now to be treated as unexploded ordnance. If this occurs, notify an immediate supervisor, refer to unit SOP for procedures regarding misfire reporting (if the tactical situation permits), and notify higher headquarters. EOD must be notified for proper disposal of a misfire.

> **DANGER**
>
> IF THE MUNITION FAILS TO INITIATE, EOD PERSONNEL MUST WAIT 30 MINUTES BEFORE APPROACHING THE MUNITION. NO OTHER PERSONNEL SHOULD APPROACH THE MUNITION.

Neither an Additional M81 Igniter nor an Additional Shock Tube Assembly With Pull Initiator is Available

2-21. If neither an M81 igniter nor an additional shock tube assembly with pull initiator is not available, the munition is now to be treated as unexploded ordnance. If this occurs, the operator notifies his supervisor, refers to unit SOP, and notifies higher headquarters. EOD must be notified for proper disposal of a misfire.

> **DANGER**
>
> IF THE MUNITION FAILS TO INITIATE, EOD PERSONNEL MUST WAIT 30 MINUTES BEFORE APPROACHING THE MUNITION. NO OTHER PERSONNEL SHOULD APPROACH THE MUNITION.

DISARMING

2-22. To disarm the munition, the operator performs the following procedures:
  (1) Check the igniter to ensure the safety pin is in place, if not—
    - Remove the M81 igniter safety pin from the bandoleer.
    - Align the pull rod safety pin hole with the safety pin hole in the body of the igniter. While holding the body of the igniter, turn the pull ring until the safety pin hole in the pull rod aligns with the safety pin hole in the body of the igniter.

- Insert the safety pin through the body of the igniter.
- Gently, spread the open ends of the safety pin, just enough to keep the safety pin from falling out.

(2) Secure the igniter to the spool.

RECOVERING

> **DANGER**
>
> THE OPERATOR SHOULD CARRY THE FIRING DEVICE ON HIS PERSON TO PREVENT ACCIDENTAL DETONATION BY A SECOND PERSON.
>
> THE OPERATOR MUST DISARM THE MUNITION BEFORE BEGINNING RECOVERY OPERATIONS.
>
> BEFORE RECOVERING THE MUNITION, THE OPERATOR MUST ENSURE THAT ITS DIRECTION HAS NOT CHANGED. IF THE DISPOSITION OF THE MUNITION HAS CHANGED, THE OPERATOR MUST NOTIFY A SUPERVISOR BEFORE GOING NEAR THE MUNITION.

2-23. To recover the munition, the operator performs the following procedures:

(1) Check the M81 igniter to ensure that the safety pin is in place.
(2) Secure the igniter to the spool.
(3) Remove the shock tube from the stake or anchor at the firing position.
(4) Wrap the shock tube around the spool, while moving toward the emplaced munition.
(5) Lay the spool down by the stake (or anchor), when you reach the emplaced munition.
(6) Observe the munition and surrounding area to check for booby traps and tampering.
(7) Remove the shipping plug priming adapter from the detonator well.

> **DANGER**
>
> ALL OPERATORS MUST WEAR LEATHER-PALMED GLOVES WHEN HANDLING BLASTING CAPS. OPERATORS MUST NOT TOUCH THE BLASTING CAP WITH THEIR BARE HANDS. THIS CAN CAUSE UNINTENTIONAL DETONATION OF THE BLASTING CAP.

(8) Remove the blasting cap and shock tube from the shipping plug priming adapter.
(9) Pick up the spool, and rest the blasting cap inside it. Place the spool back on the ground.
(10) Invert the shipping plug priming adapter, and screw the plug end of the adapter into the detonator well.
(11) Lift the munition from its emplacement, and secure the folding legs.
(12) Repack the munition in the bandoleer.
(13) Pick up the spool, and remove the shock tube from the stake (or anchor) at the munition emplacement site.
(14) Wrap the remaining shock tube around the spool and secure the blasting cap.
(15) Repack the shock tube assembly with pull initiator in the bandoleer.
(16) Move back to the firing position.
(17) Ensure that all items are packed in the bandoleer.

DESTROYING

> **DANGER**
> BEFORE USING ANY DESTRUCTION PROCEDURES, ALL SOLDIERS MUST MOVE TO A SAFE POSITION AND TAKE COVER TO AVOID POSSIBLE INJURY OR DEATH.

2-24. Destruction of any military weapon is authorized only as a last resort to prevent the enemy from capturing or using it. In combat situations, the commander has the authority to destroy weapons, but he must report doing so through the proper channels. M18A1 claymore munitions are most quickly destroyed by detonation or burning.

Notes.
1. Certain destruction procedures require the use of explosives and incendiary grenades. Related principles and the specific conditions under which destruction occurs are command decisions.
2. FM 3-34.214 provides more information about the proper procedures used for demolitions.
3. TM 43-0002-33 provides additional information regarding the destruction of military weapons.

This page intentionally left blank.

Chapter 3
Method of Initiation: M57 Firing Device

This chapter covers electrical initiation of the M18A1 claymore munition using the M57 firing device (Figure 3-1).

Note. M18A1 claymore munitions equipped with electrical firing systems will remain in the Army inventory until the current stock is exhausted.

Figure 3-1. M18A1 claymore munition with an electrical firing system

SECTION I. COMPONENTS

3-1. Besides the M18A1 claymore munition, the kit comes with the following accessories (Figure 3-2):
- M57 firing device.
- M4 electrical blasting cap assembly.
- M40 test set.
- M7 bandoleer.

Chapter 3

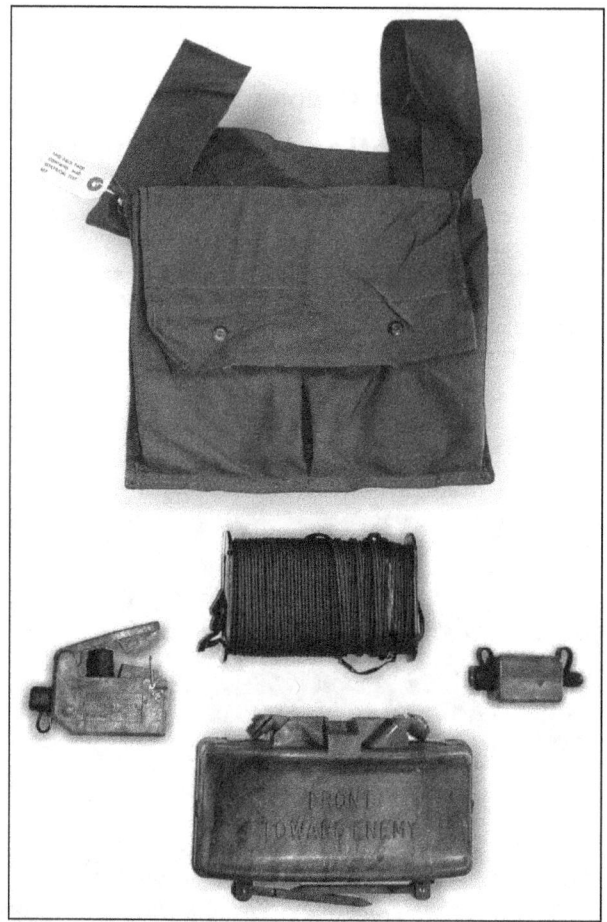

Figure 3-2. Components of the M18A1 claymore munition kit
(with an electrical firing system)

M57 FIRING DEVICE

3-2. One M57 firing device (Figure 3-3) is issued with each M18A1 claymore munition. The technical specifications for the firing device are listed in Table 3-1.

3-3. The M57 firing device is a handheld pulse generator. A squeeze of the handle produces a double (one positive, one negative) three-volt electrical pulse of energy. The 30 meters (100 feet) of firing wire issued with the munition channels this energy to fire the munition.

3-4. On one end, the M57 firing device has a rubber connecting plug with a dust cover; on the other, it has a safety bail (Figure 3-3). The safety bail has two positions: SAFE and FIRE. When it is in the SAFE position, it acts as a block between the firing handle and the pulse generator; when it is in the FIRE position, it is clear of the firing handle and allows the pulse generator to be activated.

Method of Initiation: M57 Firing Device

Notes. 1. The operator should not discard the M57 firing device and firing wire after initial use. He can attach another electrical blasting cap to the firing wire, and use the M57 firing device to fire other devices, such as breaching and demolition charges, provided that no more than 100 feet of firing wire and one blasting cap are used.

2. If the M57 firing device is damaged or fails its circuit test, the operator can use a dry-cell battery that generates 3 or more volts of power to fire the electrical blasting cap.

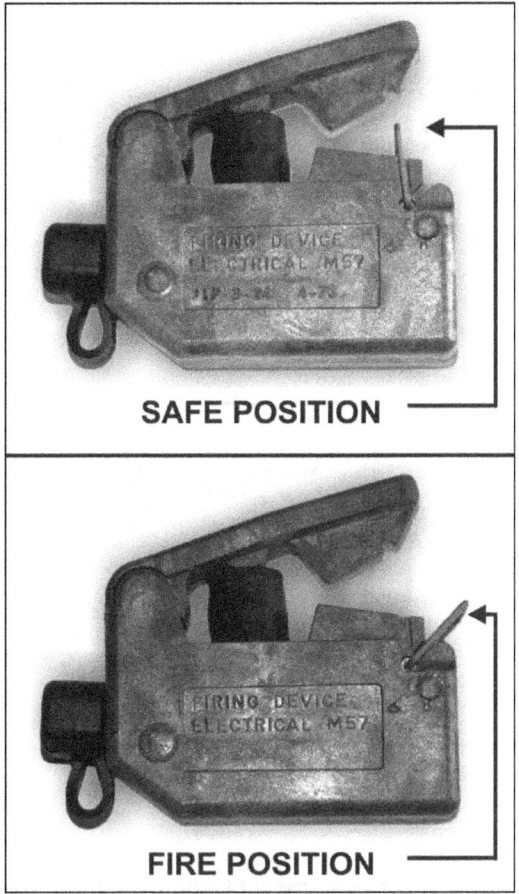

Figure 3-3. M57 firing device

Table 3-1. Technical specifications for the M57 firing device

Weight	3/4 pound
Length	4 inches
Width	1 1/2 inches
Height	3 1/4 inches

Chapter 3

M4 ELECTRICAL BLASTING CAP ASSEMBLY

3-5. The M4 electrical blasting cap assembly (Figure 3-4) consists of an M6 electrical blasting cap attached to 30 meters (100 feet) of firing wire (Figure 3-4). On one end, the firing wire has a combination shorting plug and dust cover (Figure 3-4). The shorting plug prevents accidental functioning of the blasting cap by static electricity; the dust cover prevents dirt and moisture from entering the connector. The firing wire is wrapped around a spool, with both the connector and blasting cap stored inside the spool when not in use. A piece of insulating tape is used to hold the package together.

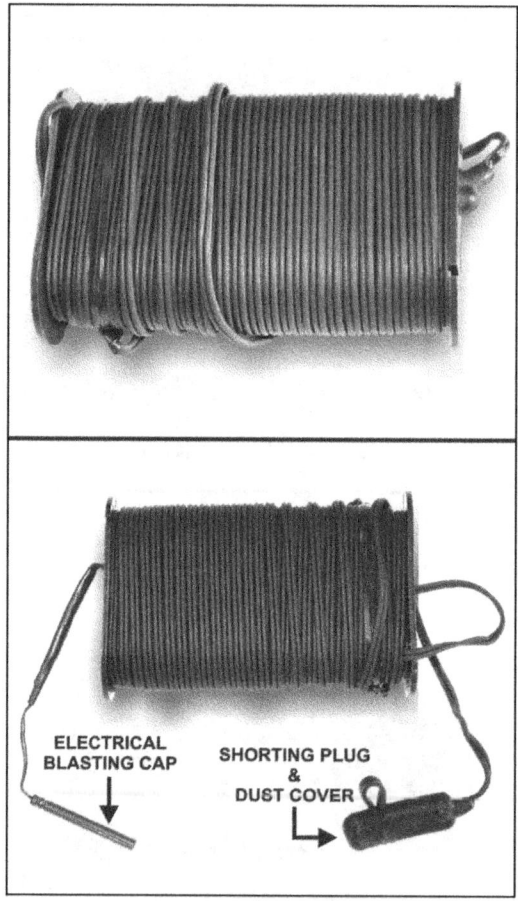

Figure 3-4. M4 electrical blasting cap assembly

Method of Initiation: M57 Firing Device

M40 TEST SET

3-6. The M40 test set (Figure 3-5) checks for continuity of the electrical firing circuit. A small window located on top of the test set allows for observing the flashes of the indicator lamp (Figure 3-5).

3-7. Table 3-2 lists the technical specifications for the test set.

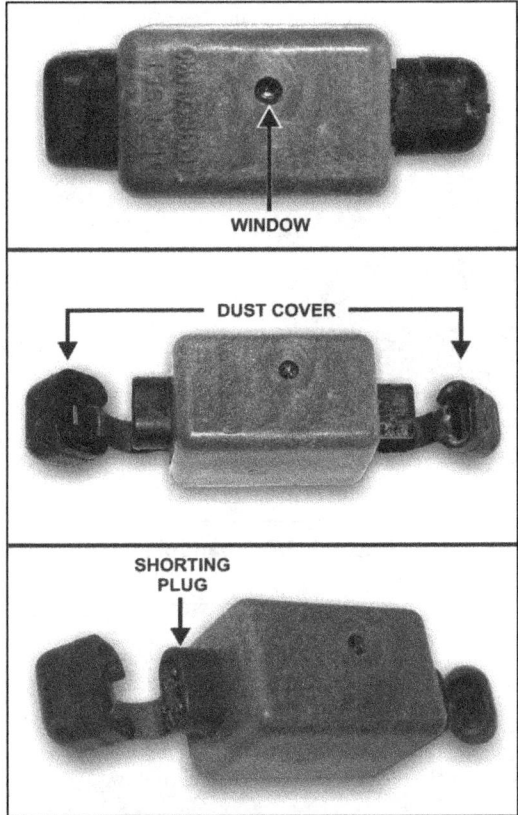

Figure 3-5. M40 test set

Table 3-2. Technical specifications for the M40 test set

Weight	8 ounces
Length	2 inches
Height	1 1/2 inches

Notes. 1. One M40 test set is provided with each case of six M18A1 claymore munitions. The bandoleer containing the test set is marked by an identification tag on the carrying strap.

2. The M40 test set should not be discarded after initial use.

Chapter 3

M7 BANDOLEER

3-8. The munition and all its accessories are carried in an M7 bandoleer (Figure 3-6). The M7 bandoleer is constructed of olive drab, water-resistant canvas and has snap fasteners to secure the flap. The bandoleer has two pockets: one pocket contains the munition, and the other contains an M57 electrical firing device, an M40 test set, and an M4 electrical blasting cap assembly. A 2-inch wide, webbed shoulder carrying strap is sewn to the bag. An instruction sheet for operation is sewn to the inside flap of the M7 bandoleer (Figure 3-7).

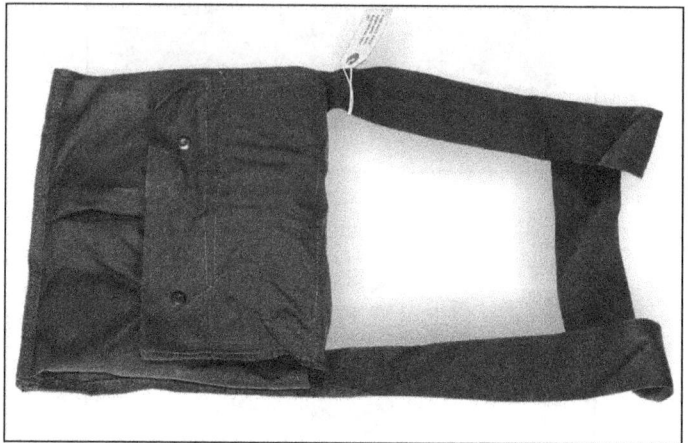

Figure 3-6. M7 bandoleer

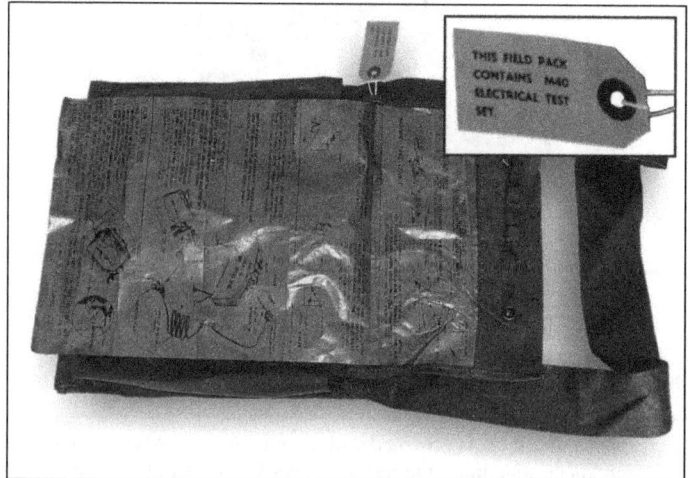

Figure 3-7. M7 bandoleer with sewn-in instructions

Method of Initiation: M57 Firing Device

SECTION II. STANDARD OPERATION

3-9. During electrical initiation, the blasting cap is detonated by squeezing the M57 firing device handle with the safety bail in the FIRE position. The detonation of the blasting cap, in turn, sets off a high-explosive charge.

> *Note.* All operators should read the instruction sheet inside of the bandoleer cover before employing the munition.

> **DANGER**
>
> ALL OPERATORS MUST WEAR LEATHER-PALMED GLOVES WHEN HANDLING BLASTING CAPS. OPERATORS MUST NOT TOUCH THE BLASTING CAP WITH THEIR BARE HANDS. THIS CAN CAUSE UNINTENTIONAL DETONATION OF THE BLASTING CAP.

3-10. With the understanding of how to employ the munition, the operator performs the following procedures:
- Select and prepare the firing position.
- Conduct a circuit test.
- Employ the munition.
- Aim the munition.
- Arm the munition.
- Camouflage the munition.
- Conduct the final circuit test.
- Fire the munition.

SELECTING AND PREPARING A FIRING POSITION

> **DANGER**
>
> FRIENDLY TROOPS ARE PROHIBITED IN AREAS TO THE REAR AND SIDES OF THE MUNITION WITHIN A RADIUS OF 16 METERS.
>
> THE MINIMUM SAFE OPERATING DISTANCE FROM THE MUNITION IS 16 METERS. AT THIS DISTANCE, THE OPERATOR MUST BE POSITIONED IN A FOXHOLE, BEHIND COVER, OR LYING PRONE IN A DEPRESSION.
>
> THE OPERATOR AND ALL FRIENDLY TROOPS WITHIN 100 METERS OF THE MUNITION MUST TAKE COVER TO PREVENT BEING INJURED BY FLYING SECONDARY OBJECTS (SUCH AS STICKS, STONES, AND PEBBLES).

3-11. The operator should select or prepare a firing position that offers cover and unobstructed observation of the site selected for emplacing the munition.

3-12. Once the operator has selected and prepared a firing position, he performs the following procedures:
  (1) Place the bandoleer on the shoulder or around the neck (Figure 3-8).
  (2) Ensure that the munition and all accessories are in the bandoleer (Figure 3-8).
  (3) Conduct a circuit test.

Chapter 3

Figure 3-8. Inspecting an M7 bandoleer packed with an M18A1 claymore munition and electrical firing system accessories

CONDUCTING A CIRCUIT TEST

3-13. The M40 test set tests the M57 firing device and the M4 electrical blasting cap assembly.

M57 FIRING DEVICE

3-14. To test the M57 firing device, the operator performs the following steps:

> **DANGER**
> THE OPERATOR SHOULD CARRY THE FIRING DEVICE ON HIS PERSON TO PREVENT ACCIDENTAL DETONATION BY A SECOND PERSON.

(1) Remove the firing device and the M40 test set from the bandoleer (Figure 3-9).
(2) Remove the dust cover from the connector of the firing device and from the connector of the test set.

(3) Check the connectors and dust covers of the firing device and test set for foreign material. Remove any dirt or debris from the connectors or dust covers by gently tapping the devices against the palm of the hand.

Note. Leave the combination shorting plug and dust cover closed on the other end of the test set.

(4) Plug the test set into the firing device (Figure 3-9).

Figure 3-9. Plugging the M40 test set into the M57 firing device

(5) Move the firing device safety bail to the FIRE position (Figure 3-10).

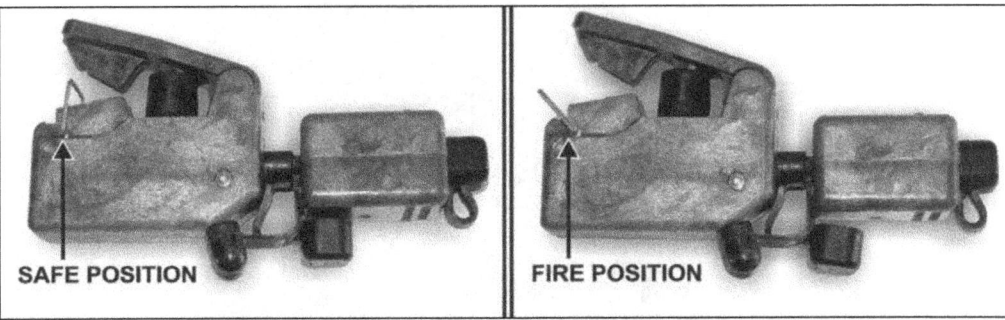

Figure 3-10. Moving the M57 firing device from the SAFE position to the FIRE position

(6) Place the eye near the window of the test set, and squeeze the handle of the firing device quickly to observe the indicator lamp flashing through the window of the test set (Figure 3-11).

Notes.   1.   The indicator lamp flashes if the firing device is functioning properly.

2. When checking the firing device and blasting cap circuitry, the operator holds the window of the test set near his eye and shades it with his other hand (Figure 3-11). This minimizes the risk of enemy observation in the dark and enables the operator to see the indicator lamp flashing, even in bright sunlight.

3. Corrosion on the electrical connectors of the test set can cause the indicator lamp to function improperly (not flash). The operator can overcome this by connecting and disconnecting the shorting plug dust cover on the M40 test set. If the test set indicates that several firing devices are faulty, he should retest with another set, since the device may be defective.

(7) Move the firing device bail to the SAFE position (Figure 3-10).
(8) Place the firing device with the test set attached in the bandoleer.

Figure 3-11. Conducting a circuit test of the M57 firing device while observing the window on the M40 test set

M4 Blasting Cap

3-15. To test the M4 electrical blasting cap assembly, the operator performs the following procedures:

> **DANGER**
>
> THE FIRING CIRCUIT TEST MUST BE CONDUCTED BEFORE PLACING THE BLASTING CAP INTO THE DETONATOR WELL. THIS PRECAUTION PREVENTS DESTRUCTION OF THE MUNITION IF THE TESTING SET MALFUNCTIONS AND DETONATES THE ELECTRICAL BLASTING CAP.

> **WARNING**
>
> If the testing set detonates the blasting cap during testing, the operator can replace it with a standard electrical blasting cap attached to the remaining firing wire.
>
> Before and after completion of the firing device and blasting cap continuity tests, the operator must ensure that the safety bail is in the SAFE position.

Notes.
1. Before performing these procedures, the operator should ensure that the firing device and test set are operative. The steps listed previously provide more information.
2. If time and circumstances do not allow for a circuit test to be conducted with the blasting cap removed from the mine, an abbreviated test may be conducted with the blasting cap inserted into the detonator well. If an abbreviated test is conducted, all personnel must be under cover at least 250 meters from the front and the sides of the mine, and 100 meters to the rear of the mine.

(1) Remove the firing wire assembly from the bandoleer.
(2) Remove the twist tie from the spool.
(3) Starting at the shorting plug/dust cover end of the electrical wire, uncoil approximately 1 meter (3 feet) of wire. To measure 1 meter of wire (Figure 3-12)—

Note. The distance from the center of the chest to one arm's length is approximately 1 meter (3 feet).

- Hold the shorting plug/dust cover against the center of the chest with the left hand.
- Encircle the firing wire at the base of the shorting plug/dust cover with the index finger and thumb of the right hand.
- While holding the right hand to the chest, extend the left hand to arm's length, allowing the firing wire to be pulled through the fingers of the right hand.
- Lock the elbow, and pull all slack from the firing wire.

Chapter 3

Figure 3-12. Unwinding approximately 1 meter (3 feet) of firing wire from spool at the firing position

(4) At the 1-meter mark, fold the firing wire to create a loop with a large enough circumference to go around the chosen stake (Figure 3-13, A).

(5) Twist the loop over the index and middle fingers of the right hand (Figure 3-13, B).

(6) Push the loop through the circle created in Step (5) (Figure 3-13, C).

(7) Secure the firing wire from the blasting cap side of the munition to a stake (Figure 3-13, D) or a fixed object at the firing position. This prevents the munition from being misaligned if the firing wire is disturbed.

Method of Initiation: M57 Firing Device

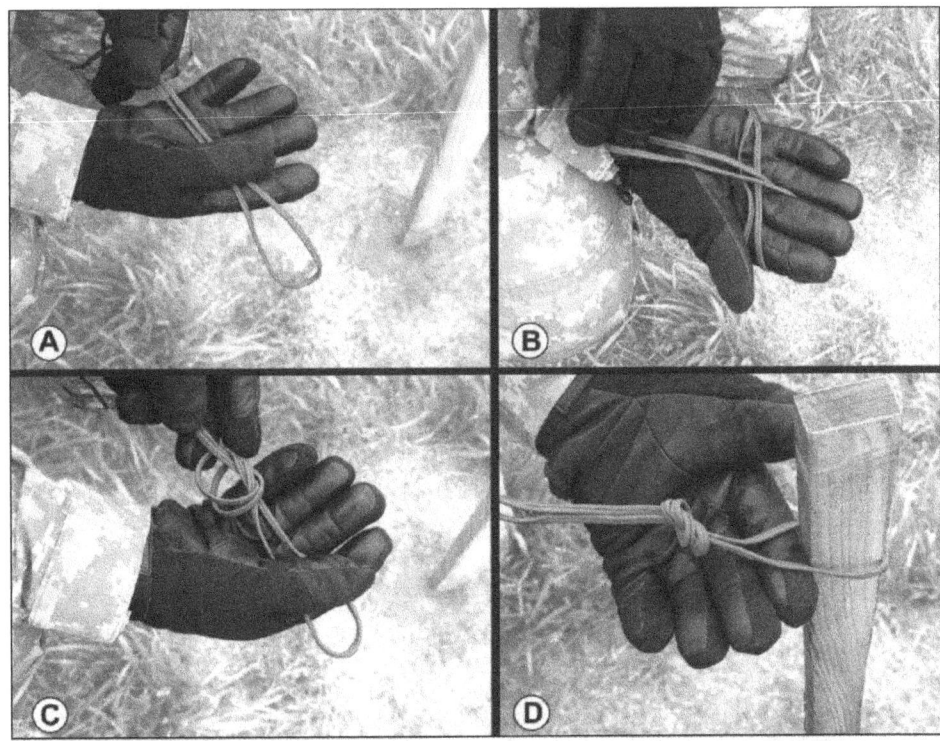

Figure 3-13. Securing firing wire at the M18A1 claymore munition firing position

> **DANGER**
>
> THE OPERATOR MUST ENSURE THAT NO FRIENDLY PERSONNEL ARE NEAR THE BLASTING CAP, AS IT MIGHT DETONATE.
>
> WHEN PERFORMING A CIRCUIT TEST, THE OPERATOR MUST PLACE THE BLASTING CAP UNDER A SANDBAG, BEHIND A TREE, OR IN A HOLE IN THE GROUND. THIS PROTECTS THE PERSON PERFORMING THE CIRCUIT TEST, SHOULD THE BLASTING CAP DETONATE.

(8) Uncoil enough wire to place the spool out of sight. Place the remaining spool of wire (with the blasting cap inside the spool) under a sandbag, behind a tree, or in a hole in the ground to protect oneself, should the blasting cap detonate (Figure 3-14).

Figure 3-14. Placing the firing wire spool (with the blasting cap) under a sandbag

(9) Remove the firing device with the test set attached from the bandoleer.
(10) Remove the shorting plug/dust cover from the connector of the firing wire and from the end of the test set.
(11) Plug the connector of the firing wire into the test set (Figure 3-15).
(12) Move the firing device safety bail to the FIRE position (Figure 3-16).
(13) Place the eye near the window of the test set, and squeeze the handle of the firing device quickly to observe the indicator lamp flashing through the window of the test set (Figure 3-17).

Figure 3-15. Plugging the firing wire connector into the M40 test set

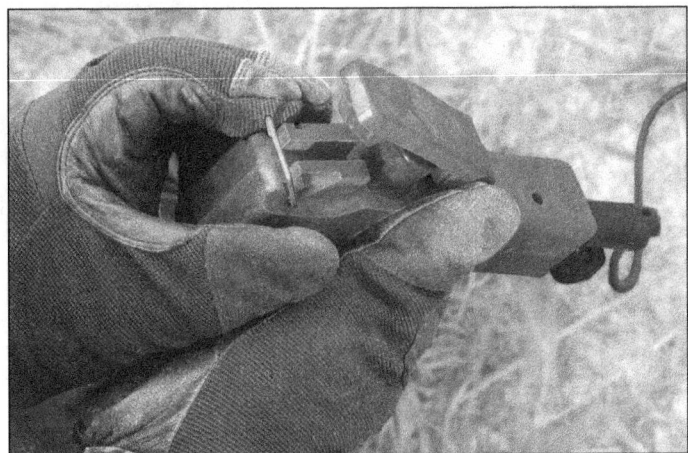

Figure 3-16. Moving the M57 firing device from the SAFE position to the FIRE position

Figure 3-17. Conducting a circuit test of the firing wire while observing the window on the M40 test set

Note. When squeezing the handle of the firing device, an indicator lamp in the window of the test set flashes. This flash indicates that the blasting cap circuitry is satisfactory. If the lamp does not flash, the operator should notify a supervisor. TM 9-1345-203-12 provides more information about troubleshooting procedures.

(14) Move the firing device bail from the FIRE position to the SAFE position.
(15) Disconnect the test set from the firing wire, and replace the firing wire and test set shorting plug/dust covers.
(16) Disconnect the test set from the firing device, and replace the firing device and test set dust covers.
(17) Repack the firing device and test set in the bandoleer.

Note. If an extended period of time elapses between the circuit test and the insertion of the blasting cap into the detonator well, or if the area is subjected to artillery or mortar fire, the operator should conduct another test.

> **DANGER**
>
> IF AN ABBREVIATED TEST IS CONDUCTED, ALL PERSONNEL MUST BE UNDER COVER AT LEAST 250 METERS AWAY FROM THE FRONT AND SIDES OF THE MUNITION, AND 100 METERS TO THE REAR OF THE MUNITION.
>
> ALL OPERATORS MUST WEAR LEATHER-PALMED GLOVES WHEN HANDLING BLASTING CAPS. OPERATORS MUST NOT TOUCH THE BLASTING CAP WITH THEIR BARE HANDS. THIS CAN CAUSE UNINTENTIONAL DETONATION OF THE BLASTING CAP.

3-16. If time and circumstances do not allow for a circuit test to be conducted with the blasting cap removed from the mine, an abbreviated test may be conducted with the blasting cap inserted into the detonator well. If an abbreviated test is conducted, all personnel must be under cover at least 250 meters from the front and the sides of the mine, and 100 meters to the rear of the mine.

EMPLOYING

3-17. To employ the munition, the operator performs the following steps:

> **DANGER**
>
> THE OPERATOR MUST CARRY THE FIRING DEVICE ON HIS PERSON TO PREVENT ACCIDENTAL DETONATION BY A SECOND PERSON.
>
> ALL OPERATORS MUST WEAR LEATHER-PALMED GLOVES WHEN HANDLING BLASTING CAPS. OPERATORS MUST NOT TOUCH THE BLASTING CAP WITH THEIR BARE HANDS. THIS CAN CAUSE UNINTENTIONAL DETONATION OF THE BLASTING CAP.

> **WARNING**
>
> The operator should ensure that the combination shorting plug and dust cover is assembled to the connector of the firing wire before proceeding with installation of the munition.

Note. The operator should ensure the M57 firing device and M40 test set are in the bandoleer before leaving the firing position.

(1) Remove the spool with the remaining firing wire and blasting cap from the protective barrier used during circuit testing of the electrical wire.
(2) Unroll the firing wire from the firing position to the site selected for munition emplacement (Figure 3-18).

Notes. 1. Chapter 5 provides more information about selecting a site for munition emplacement.
2. The blasting cap end of the firing wire is on the inside of the spool.

Figure 3-18. Unwinding firing wire from the spool while moving toward the munition emplacement site

(3) Lay the spool (with the blasting cap inside) down within arm's reach of the munition emplacement site.

(4) Remove the munition from the bandoleer.

(5) Turn the legs rearward and then downward.
(6) Spread each pair of legs approximately 45 degrees.

Note. One leg should protrude to the front of the munition, and one to the rear of the munition (Figure 3-19).

Figure 3-19. Preparing the M18A1 claymore munition for emplacement

DANGER
THE OPERATOR MUST ENSURE THAT THE MUNITION IS POSITIONED WITH THE SURFACE MARKED "FRONT TOWARD ENEMY" AND THE ARROWS ON TOP OF THE MUNITION POINTING IN THE DIRECTION OF THE ENEMY OR THE DESIRED AREA OF FIRE.

(7) Position the munition with the surface marked "FRONT TOWARD ENEMY" and the arrows on top of the munition pointing in the direction of the enemy or the desired area of fire (Figure 3-20).
(8) Press the legs approximately 1/3 of the way into the ground.

Note. To prevent tipping in windy areas or when the legs cannot be pressed into the ground, the operator should spread the legs to the maximum breadth (approximately 180 degrees so that the legs are to the front and rear of the munition). On snow or extremely soft ground, the operator may spread the bandoleer beneath the mine for support.

(9) Aim the munition (Figure 3-20).

Figure 3-20. Positioning the M18A1 claymore munition with the front facing in the desired area of fire

Chapter 3

AIMING

3-18. To aim the munitions (Figure 3-21), the operator performs the following procedures:
  (1) Select an aiming point that is at ground level and approximately 50 meters (150 feet) in front of the munition.
  (2) Position the eye approximately 6 inches (15 centimeters) to the rear of the sight.
  (3) Aim the munition by aligning the two edges of the sight with the aiming point.

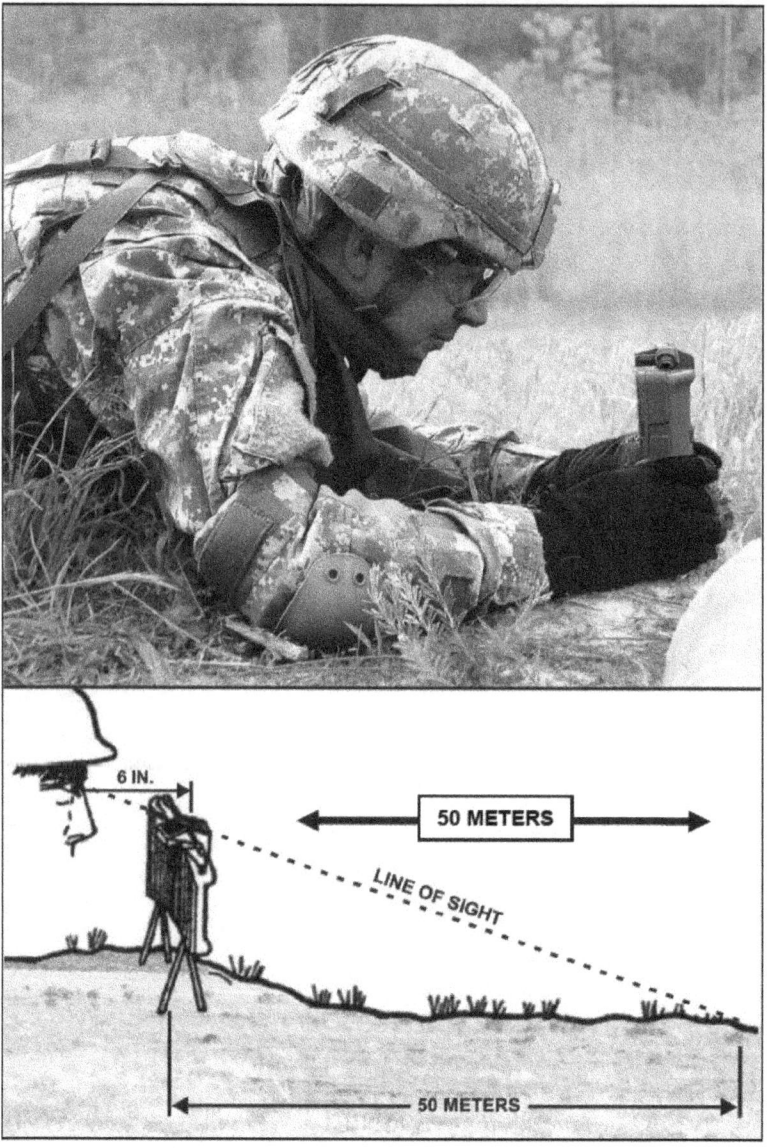

Figure 3-21. Aiming an M18A1 claymore munition

ARMING

3-19. To arm the munition, the operator performs the following procedures:

> **DANGER**
>
> THE OPERATOR MUST NOT INSERT THE BLASTING CAP INTO THE DETONATOR WELL UNTIL HE HAS EMPLACED AND AIMED THE MUNITION.
>
> ALL OPERATORS MUST WEAR LEATHER-PALMED GLOVES WHEN HANDLING BLASTING CAPS. OPERATORS MUST NOT TOUCH THE BLASTING CAP WITH THEIR BARE HANDS. THIS CAN CAUSE UNINTENTIONAL DETONATION OF THE BLASTING CAP.

(1) Recover the spool, and remove the blasting cap from the spool's cavity.

(2) Secure the firing wire (Figure 3-22) approximately 1 meter from the blasting cap side of the munition to a stake, a stone, gravel, a sand bag, or another available means. This prevents the munition from being misaligned if the firing wire is disturbed.

Note. To perform Step (2), the operator follows the same procedures used to secure the firing wire at the firing position.

Figure 3-22. Securing the firing wire at the munition emplacement site

(3) Unscrew and invert the shipping plug priming adapter nearest to the stake or anchor (Figure 3-23, A).

(4) Slide the slotted end of the shipping plug priming adapter approximately 1 inch onto the firing wire between the crimped connections and the blasting cap (Figure 3-23, B).

(5) Pull the firing wire through the shipping plug priming adapter until the top of the blasting cap is firmly seated in the bottom portion of the shipping plug priming adapter (Figure 3-23, C).

(6) Insert the blasting cap, and screw the adapter into the detonator well (Figure 3-23, D).

Chapter 3

Figure 3-23. Arming the M18A1 claymore munition equipped with an electrical firing system

(7) Re-aim the munition to ensure that the point of aim has not changed (Figure 3-24).

Figure 3-24. Re-aiming an employed M18A1 claymore munition

Method of Initiation: M57 Firing Device

Notes. 1. The operator leaves the spool at the firing site, beside the stake or anchor.

2. If there is nothing on which to secure the wire, the operator wraps it twice around the base of the munition, and then place the spool in front of the munition's base (Figure 3-25).

3. The firing procedures provide more information.

Figure 3-25. Placing the firing wire spool with remainder of spooled wire in front of the M18A1 claymore munition

DANGER
THE OPERATOR SHOULD CARRY THE FIRING DEVICE ON HIS PERSON TO PREVENT ACCIDENTAL DETONATION BY A SECOND PERSON.

Note: The operator camouflages the munition before leaving the emplacement site, and camouflages the firing wire as he returns to his firing position. The following section provides more information about camouflage.

(8) Ensure you have the bandoleer and other accessories, and return to the firing position.

CAMOUFLAGING

> **WARNING**
>
> When camouflaging the munition, the operator uses only lightweight foliage, such as leaves and grass, to avoid increasing the secondary missile hazard to the rear of the munition.

3-20. Although the M18A1 claymore munition is painted olive drab to facilitate camouflaging, the operator must ensure to blend it into its surroundings to prevent detection. Both the front and rear of the munition should be camouflaged with foliage. The firing wire should also be camouflaged or buried underground. If used (as is common with dual priming), the time fuze attached to detonating cord can be buried or covered with light foliage.

Note. TC 3-21.75 outlines the principles and methods of camouflage. TM 9-1345-203-12 provides more information about the use of time fuzes attached to detonating cord for dual priming.

CONDUCTING A FINAL CIRCUIT TEST

3-21. Before firing the mine, the operator conducts a final circuit test. This test verifies that the circuit has not been broken during emplacement. This test is similar to the initial circuit test, and it should be conducted if time and circumstances allow. To perform a final circuit test, the operator performs the following procedures:

> **DANGER**
>
> WHEN A FINAL CIRCUIT TEST IS CONDUCTED, ALL PERSONNEL MUST BE UNDER COVER AT LEAST 250 METERS AWAY FROM THE FRONT AND SIDES OF THE MUNITION, AND 100 METERS TO THE REAR OF THE MUNITION.

(1) Seek cover.
(2) Remove the firing device and the test set from the bandoleer.
(3) Remove the dust cover from the connector of the firing device and from the connector of the test set.
(4) Plug the test set into the firing device.
(5) Remove the shorting plug/dust cover from the connector of the firing wire and from the end of the test set.
(6) Plug the connector of the firing wire into the test set.
(7) Move the firing device safety bail to the FIRE position.
(8) Place the eye near the window of the test set, and squeeze the handle of the firing device quickly to observe the indicator lamp flashing through the window of the test set.

Note. When squeezing the handle of the firing device, the operator will see a flash in the indicator lamp in the window of the test set. This flash indicates that the blasting cap circuitry is satisfactory. If the lamp does not flash, the operator must notify his supervisor. TM 9-1345-203-12 provides more information about troubleshooting procedures.

(9) Move the firing device bail from the FIRE position to the SAFE position.

(10) Disconnect the test set from the firing wire, and replace the firing wire and test set shorting plug/dust covers.
(11) Disconnect the test set from the firing device, and replace the firing device and test set dust covers.
(12) Repack the firing device and test set in the bandoleer.

Note. If an extended period elapses between the final circuit test and munition employment or if the area is subjected to artillery or mortar fire, the operator should conduct another test.

FIRING

> **WARNING**
>
> Before detonating an M18A1 claymore munition, operators must use appropriate hearing protection. Single hearing protection is required for all personnel within 90 meters (300 feet) of the munition.

> **DANGER**
>
> THE OPERATOR MUST NOT CONNECT THE FIRING DEVICE TO THE FIRING WIRE UNTIL THE ACTUAL TIME OF FIRING.
>
> BEFORE CONNECTING THE M57 FIRING DEVICE TO THE FIRING WIRE, THE OPERATOR MUST ENSURE THAT THE SAFETY BAIL IS IN THE SAFE POSITION AND THAT ALL FRIENDLY TROOPS WITHIN 250 METERS OF THE FRONT AND SIDES, AND 100 METERS OF THE REAR OF THE MUNITION ARE UNDER COVER.

3-22. To fire the munition, the operator performs the following procedures:
(1) Seek cover.
(2) Remove the dust cover on the firing device.
(3) Remove the shorting plug/dust cover from the end of the firing wire.
(4) Connect the firing device to the firing wire (Figure 3-26, A).

Note. Tactical situations may dictate the performance of Step (5).

(5) Alert friendly personnel by announcing "CLAYMORE" twice (depending on the situation).
(6) Move the firing device safety bail to the FIRE position (Figure 3-26, B) and quickly squeeze the firing device handle (Figure 3-26, C).

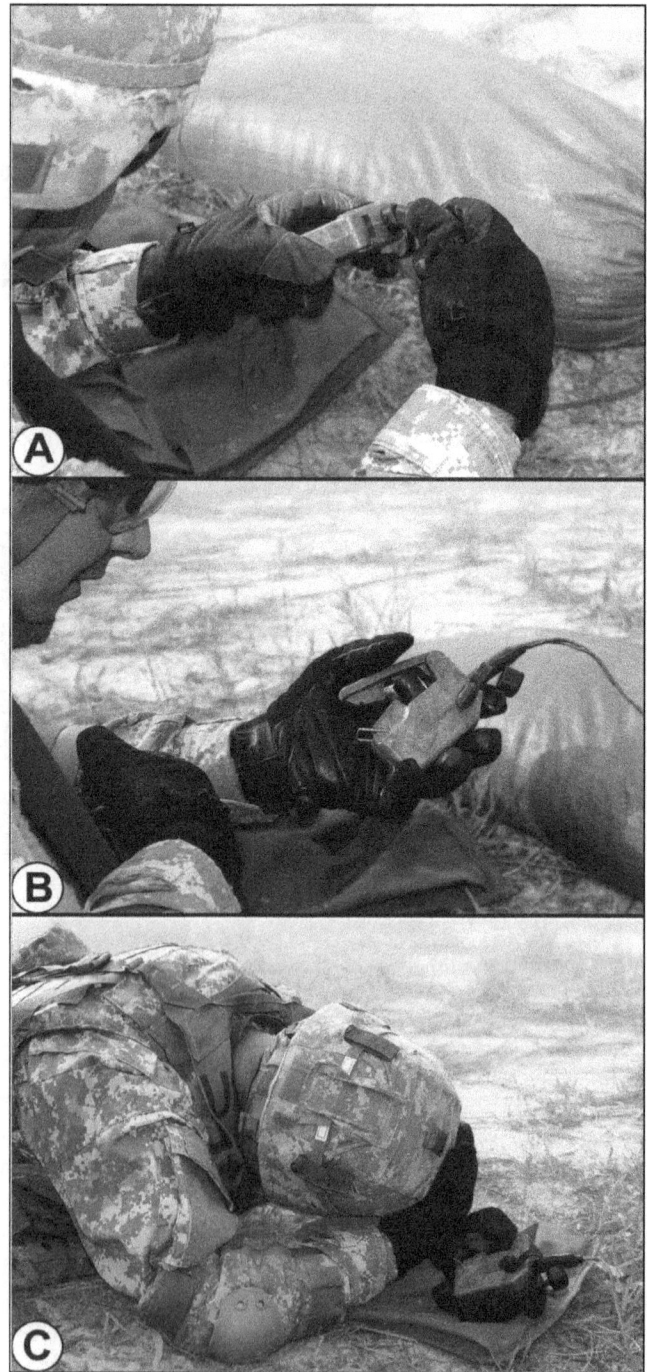

Figure 3-26. Firing an M18A1 claymore munition with an M57 firing device

Method of Initiation: M57 Firing Device

SECTION III. OPERATION UNDER UNUSUAL CONDITIONS

3-23. Operators must be capable of employing M18A1 claymore munitions under various operational conditions. Operators may also encounter events that change normal operation of the munition, such as misfires. Further, other situations may require disarming, recovering, or destroying the munition.

ADDRESSING A MISFIRE

3-24. A misfire is a complete failure to fire caused by a procedural or mechanical failure.

Note. The operator must notify his supervisor and ammunition supply point (ASP) of any unusual occurrence, regardless of whether the munition fires or not.

3-25. The procedures vary according to the type of mission: operational or training.

OPERATIONAL MISSION

3-26. If the munition fails to function after the operator has squeezed the handle of the firing device, he performs the following procedures:
  (1) If the munition is dual-primed, attempt to fire using the secondary initiation device. If the munition still fails to fire, continue using the following procedures.
  (2) Attempt to fire again.
  (3) Check the connection between the firing device and the firing wire.
  (4) Attempt to fire again.
  (5) If the munition fails to function again, announce "MISFIRE" three times (depending on the situation).
  (6) Using the M40 test set, check the continuity of the electrical firing circuit.
  (7) Attempt to fire again.

Note. Tactical situations may dictate the performance of Step (8).

  (8) If the munition fails to function again, announce "MISFIRE" three times (depending on the situation).
  (9) If the blasting cap assembly activates but the munition fails to function, the munition is now to be treated as unexploded ordnance. If this occurs, notify a supervisor, refer to unit SOP, and notify higher headquarters. EOD must be notified for proper disposal of a misfire.

DANGER

IF THE MUNITION FAILS TO INITIATE, EOD PERSONNEL MUST WAIT 30 MINUTES BEFORE APPROACHING THE MUNITION. NO OTHER PERSONNEL SHOULD APPROACH THE MUNITION.

TRAINING

3-27. If the munition fails to function after the operator has squeezed the handle of the firing device, he performs the following procedures:
  (1) If the munition is dual-primed, attempt to fire using the secondary initiation device. If the munition still fails to fire, continue using the following procedures.
  (2) Announce "MISFIRE" three times.
  (3) Attempt to fire again.
  (4) If the munition fails to function again, announce "MISFIRE" three times.

(5) Check the connection between the firing device and the firing wire.
(6) Attempt to fire again.
(7) If the munition fails to function again, announce "MISFIRE" three times.
(8) Using the M40 test set, check the continuity of the electrical firing circuit.
(9) Attempt to fire again.
(10) If the munition fails to function again, announce "MISFIRE" three times.
(11) If the blasting cap assembly activates but the munition fails to function, the munition is now to be treated as unexploded ordnance. If this occurs, notify a supervisor, refer to unit SOP, and notify higher headquarters. EOD must be notified for proper disposal of a misfire.

> **DANGER**
>
> IF THE MUNITION FAILS TO INITIATE, EOD PERSONNEL MUST WAIT 30 MINUTES BEFORE APPROACHING THE MUNITION. NO OTHER PERSONNEL SHOULD APPROACH THE MUNITION.

DISARMING

3-28. To disarm the munition, the operator performs the following procedures:

> **DANGER**
>
> BEFORE DISARMING THE MUNITION, THE OPERATOR ENSURES THAT THE SAFETY BAIL IS IN THE SAFE POSITION AND THAT ALL FRIENDLY TROOPS WITHIN 250 METERS OF THE FRONT AND SIDES, AND 100 METERS OF THE REAR OF THE MUNITION ARE UNDER COVER.

(1) Ensure the firing device safety bail is in the SAFE position.
(2) Disconnect the firing wire from the firing device.
(3) Replace the combination shorting plug dust cover on the firing wire connector and the dust cover on the firing device connector.

> **DANGER**
>
> THE OPERATOR SHOULD CARRY THE FIRING DEVICE ON HIS PERSON TO PREVENT ACCIDENTAL DETONATION BY A SECOND PERSON.

(4) Place the firing device in bandoleer.
(5) Remove the firing wire from the stake or anchor at the firing position, and place the firing wire forward of the position.

RECOVERING

> **DANGER**
> THE OPERATOR SHOULD CARRY THE FIRING DEVICE ON HIS PERSON TO PREVENT ACCIDENTAL DETONATION BY A SECOND PERSON.

3-29. To recover the munition, the operator performs the following procedures:

> **DANGER**
> THE OPERATOR MUST DISARM THE MUNITION BEFORE BEGINNING RECOVERY OPERATIONS.
>
> BEFORE RECOVERING THE MUNITION, THE OPERATOR MUST ENSURE THAT ITS DIRECTION HAS NOT CHANGED. IF THE DISPOSITION OF THE MUNITION HAS CHANGED, THE OPERATOR MUST NOTIFY A SUPERVISOR BEFORE APPROACHING THE MUNITION.

(1) Move to the M18A1 claymore munition.
(2) Observe the munition and surrounding area to check for booby traps and tampering.
(3) Unscrew and remove the shipping plug priming adapter from the detonator well.

> **DANGER**
> ALL OPERATORS MUST WEAR LEATHER-PALMED GLOVES WHEN HANDLING BLASTING CAPS. OPERATORS MUST NOT TOUCH THE BLASTING CAP WITH THEIR BARE HANDS. THIS CAN CAUSE UNINTENTIONAL DETONATION OF THE BLASTING CAP.

(4) Remove the blasting cap and firing wire from the shipping plug priming adapter.
(5) Pick up the spool, and insert the blasting cap inside it. Place the spool back on the ground.
(6) Invert the shipping plug priming adapter, and screw the plug end of the adapter into the detonator well.
(7) Remove the firing wire from the stake, anchor, or base of the emplaced munition.
(8) Lift the munition from its emplacement, and secure the folding legs.
(9) Repack the munition in the bandoleer.
(10) Pick up the spool. Wrap the firing wire on the spool as you move back to the firing position, and secure the shorting plug and dust cover inside the spool.
(11) Repack the electrical wire assembly in the bandoleer.
(12) Ensure the munition, M57 firing device, and the M40 test set are packed in the bandoleer.

Chapter 3

DESTROYING

> **DANGER**
> BEFORE USING ANY DESTRUCTION PROCEDURE, ALL SOLDIERS MUST MOVE TO A SAFE POSITION AND TAKE COVER TO AVOID POSSIBLE INJURY OR DEATH.

3-30. The commander can authorize destruction of any military weapon only as a last resort to prevent the enemy from capturing or using it. In combat situations he must report doing so through the proper channels. M18A1 claymore munitions are most quickly destroyed by detonation or burning.

Notes.
1. Certain procedures require the use of explosives and incendiary grenades. Related principles and the specific conditions under which destruction occurs are command decisions.

2. FM 3-34.214 provides more information about the proper procedures used for demolitions.

3. TM 43-0002-33 provides additional information regarding the destruction of military weapons.

Chapter 4
Training

The training outlined in this chapter fully prepares Soldiers to employ M18A1 claymore munitions effectively in combat.

PHASES OF TRAINING

4-1. Training is divided into two phases: Phase I and Phase II.

PHASE I TRAINING

4-2. Phase I training familiarizes Soldiers with the characteristics, capabilities, and installation of M18A1 claymore munitions. It introduces the basic skills necessary to employ M18A1 claymore munitions. Further, it addresses conventional munition detonation methods using nonelectrical and electrical firing systems in the controlled role.

Elements

4-3. Soldiers receive training in the following areas:
- Characteristics and capabilities of M18A1 claymore munitions.
- Safety procedures.
- Sequence of installation, aiming, and arming.
- Camouflage techniques.
- Misfire.
- Disarming.
- Recovery.
- Destruction.
- Tactical employment.
- Simulated employment and recovery of a training aid.

Note. Chapters 2 and 3 of this book and TM 9-1345-203-12 provide more information about these areas.

Practical Exercises

4-4. Trainers should emphasize practical exercises using inert or simulated munitions.

Note. These items can be obtained from local training support centers (TSCs).

PHASE II TRAINING

4-5. During Phase II training, Soldiers receive instruction on unconventional munition detonation methods using nonelectrical firing systems in the controlled role, tactical employment, and other advanced training.

Note. M18A1 claymore munitions equipped with electrical firing systems will remain in the Army inventory until the current stock is exhausted. Commanders are encouraged to train Soldiers on the use of nonelectrical and electrical firing systems.

Chapter 4

Elements

4-6. Soldiers receive training in the following areas:
- Controlled initiation.
- Dual firing systems.
- Ring main systems.
- Tactical employment.

Note. Chapter 5 of this publication, FM 3-34.214, and TM 9-1345-203-12 provide more information about these areas.

Practical Exercises

4-7. Initially, trainers should conduct practical exercises using inert or practice munitions. Soldiers become more proficient, training progresses to the use of live explosives. Trainers should also use practical exercises to emphasize employment of munitions in various tactical situations.

SUSTAINMENT TRAINING

4-8. To maintain proficiency after completing Phase I and Phase II training, Soldiers should employ inert munitions in both the conventional and unconventional roles during field training.

TRAINING AIDS

4-9. Training aids should be used during Phase I and Phase II training. Effective training aids improve instruction and increase understanding. For example, a model, picture, or chart can be used to explain how the munition functions or is installed.

Note. Wherever possible, local TSCs should be used to obtain desired training aids and devices. These centers loan and/or fabricate the required aids and devices.

4-10. Other instructional resources include—
- 071-325-4425 (IMI), Deploy an M18A1 Claymore Mine (interactive multimedia instruction).
- 071-325-4426 (IMI), Recover an M18A1 Claymore Mine (interactive multimedia instruction).

INSTRUCTORS/TRAINERS

4-11. Knowledgeable instructors or cadre are the key to the safe handling and employment of M18A1 claymore munitions. All commanders should strive to maintain expertise in M18A1 claymore munition instruction and training according to training circulars (TCs), field manuals (FMs), technical manuals (TMs), Army regulations (ARs), and command standard operating procedures (SOPs).

SELECTION

4-12. Team, squad, and section leaders and platoon sergeants are trainers within a unit. These Soldiers must—
- Demonstrate proficiency in all aspects of M18A1 claymore munition employment.
- Have employed live M18A1 claymore munitions.
- Demonstrate competence and a professional attitude.

4-13. Before becoming trainers, they must be assessed carefully and their shortcomings must be corrected. The commander chooses a method of assessing the trainers that accurately evaluates their abilities. With the assistance of unit senior trainers (command sergeants major and company first sergeants), platoon leaders, and platoon sergeants, the commander performs the assessment.

DUTIES

4-14. Instructors/trainers help Soldiers master the fundamentals of M18A1 claymore munition employment. They ensure that Soldiers consistently apply what they have learned. They must also perform the following tasks:
- Set up and run a range.
- Conduct an orientation safety briefing.
- Inspect the M18A1 claymore munition for serviceability.
- Prepare the M18A1 claymore munition for firing.
- Demonstrate the correct firing positions.
- Estimate range.
- Obtain the correct sight alignment.
- Perform the correct combat and training misfire procedures.
- Disarm the M18A1 claymore munition.
- Recover the M18A1 claymore munition.

TRAINING PREPARATION

4-15. Training preparation involves three steps:
(1) Conduct a training risk assessment.
(2) Conduct an environmental risk assessment.
(3) Make range coordinations.

CONDUCT A TRAINING RISK ASSESSMENT

4-16. The officer in charge (OIC) or noncommissioned officer in charge (NCOIC) conducts a training risk assessment to identify unnecessary risks by comparing potential benefit to potential loss. The risk management process allows units to identify and control hazards, conserve combat power and resources, and complete the mission. This process is cyclic and continuous; it must be integrated into all phases of operations and training.

4-17. There are five steps to the risk management process:
(1) Identify hazards.
(2) Assess hazards to determine risk.
(3) Develop controls and make risk decisions.
(4) Implement controls.
(5) Supervise and evaluate.

Notes. 1. Risk decisions must be made at the appropriate level.
2. FM 5-19 provides more information.

Identify Hazards

4-18. When identifying hazards, leaders should consider—
- The lethality of M18A1 claymore munitions.
- The area in which training is to be conducted.
- How the addition of new elements impacts known hazards.

Surface Danger Zones

4-19. Surface danger zones (SDZs) are exclusion areas identified to protect personnel from the munitions fired during training. Each SDZ contains two areas—
- Backblast danger area.
- Downrange danger area.

Chapter 4

> **DANGER**
> DURING TRAINING, THE ENTIRE BACKBLAST AREA MUST BE MARKED OFF AND KEPT CLEAR OF PERSONNEL, EQUIPMENT, AND OBSTRUCTIONS.

Notes.
1. When M18A1 claymore munitions are fired, the concussive blast of the munition creates secondary missile hazards, which are launched from the back of the munition with tremendous force. The resulting backblast can damage equipment or seriously injure personnel who are positioned too close to the rear of the munition.
2. Chapter 1 outlines live fire safety requirements.

Assess Hazards To Determine Risk

4-20. Once identified, a hazard is assessed by considering the likelihood of its occurrence and the severity of injury if no control measures are implemented. When assessing hazards, leaders should consider the Soldiers' current state of training.

Develop Controls and Make Risk Decisions

4-21. Leaders must apply two types of control measures to risk assessments:
- Educational controls.
- Physical controls.

4-22. The unit commander's controls should be clear, concise, executable orders.

Note. Most vital to developing risk management controls is mature, educated leadership.

Educational Controls

4-23. Educational controls occur when adequate training takes place. They require the largest amount of planning and training time. Leaders implement educational controls using two sequential steps:
(1) Supervisors and instructors must be certified.
(2) Soldier training must be executed.

Physical Controls

4-24. Physical controls are the measures emplaced to reduce injuries. This includes not only protective equipment, but also certified personnel to supervise the training. Unrestrained physical controls are, in themselves, a hazard.

Implement Controls

4-25. When leaders implement the controls, they must match the controls to the Soldier's skill level. They must also enforce every control measure as a means of validating its adequacy.

Supervise and Evaluate

4-26. During this step, leaders eliminate unnecessary risk and ineffective controls by identifying unexpected hazards and determining if the implemented controls reduced the residual risk without interfering with the training.

CONDUCT AN ENVIRONMENTAL RISK ASSESSMENT

4-27. All leaders, trainers, and Soldiers must comply with environmental laws and regulations. The leader must identify the environmental risks associated with training individual and collective tasks, and implement environmental protection measures by integrating them into plans, orders, SOPs, training performance standards, and rehearsals.

4-28. Environmental risk management parallels safety risk management and is based on the same philosophy. Environmental risk management consists of identifying hazards before they happen and assessing hazards caused during training.

Note. FM 5-19 provides more information.

Identify Hazards

4-29. Leaders should identify the potential sources for environmental degradation during the analysis of mission, enemy, terrain and weather, troops and support available, time available, and civil considerations (METT-TC). An environmental hazard is a condition with the potential for polluting air, soil, or water or destroying cultural or historical artifacts.

Assess Hazards

4-30. Leaders should analyze the potential severity of environmental degradation by using the environmental risk assessment matrixes in FM 5-19. Leaders quantify the environmental risk resulting from the operation as extremely high, medium, or low using the environmental risk assessment matrixes.

RANGE COORDINATIONS

4-31. Once the risk assessment is completed, viewed, and command-approved, the OIC or NCOIC should check out the range and coordinate for range use.

Note. The OIC or NCOIC should coordinate at least one day ahead of actual use to rehearse range setup and conduct.

RANGES

4-32. M18A1 claymore munition training requires a range complex that meets specific standards.

Note. TC 25-8 provides more information about ranges.

EQUIPMENT

4-33. The following list includes the minimum amount of range materiel and supplies needed to operate a practice- or live-fire event on an M18A1 claymore munition range:
- A helmet, a body armor vest, load-bearing equipment, and ear protection for all range personnel and Soldiers attending training.
- Appropriate publications pertaining to training (FMs, TMs, ARs, SOPs).
- Range flag.
- Communications equipment.
- M18A1 claymore munitions, as needed.
- Training aids, devices, simulators, and simulations (TADSS), as needed.

Note. TADSS enable Soldiers to learn as much as they can about a munition before they attempt to fire the actual munition. Their use saves money and time, and prevents injuries. A local TSC can provide more information about TADSS.

- Ambulance or required dedicated evacuation vehicle.

Note. The driver must know the route to the hospital.

- Potable water.

Chapter 4

PERSONNEL

4-34. In accordance with DA Pam 385-63, the following safety personnel are required for M18A1 claymore munition training:
- OIC.
- Range safety officer (RSO).

Note. OICs and RSOs involved in serious range incidents may lose their certification if determined to be in violation of AR 385-63 or DA Pam 385-63. While an incident is under investigation, their certificate may be suspended for as long as deemed necessary or revoked by the installation commander.

4-35. Safe and successful performance of training also requires experienced support personnel. Support personnel required for training include—
- Safety NCOs.
- Ammunition personnel.
- Tower operator.
- Guards, as required.
- Medical personnel.
- Truck driver, if applicable.

Officer in Charge and Noncommissioned Officer in Charge

4-36. The OIC must have satisfactorily completed a standard program of instruction on the duties of the OIC (developed by the unit to which he is assigned) and attended a range safety briefing conducted by the installation range control. The OIC or NCOIC must—
- Be knowledgeable in the training involved and the duties required.
- Be certified by the commander.

Note. Unit policies and regulations determine the rank of the OIC.

4-37. Once selected by the commander, the OIC should select the right personnel to conduct the training. Next, he should appoint an NCOIC who has current experience in the use of M18A1 claymore munitions. The OIC and NCOIC should—
- Select and brief range support personnel on their expected duties.
- Certify selected range personnel on their range duties.

Note. Before conducting training, the OIC and NCOIC should review unit SOPs, AR 385-63, and DA Pam 385-63.

Range Safety Officer

4-38. The RSO should be the senior M18A1 claymore munition instructor. The RSO must have satisfactorily completed a standard program of instruction in the duties of RSO (developed by the unit to which he is assigned) and attended a range safety briefing conducted by the installation range control. The RSO must—
- Be an E6 or above.
- Be knowledgeable in the munitions involved and the duties required.
- Ensure that the OIC has current safety cards.
- Perform no duties other than those of RSO.

Safety Noncommissioned Officers

4-39. Safety NCOs provide instruction and conduct safe training using practice and live M18A1 claymore munitions. Safety NCOs should—

- Be an E5 or above.
- Be knowledgeable in the munitions involved and the duties required.
- Be selected and certified on all M18A1 claymore munition tasks by the OIC and NCOIC.
- Ensure that no Soldiers are inside of the safety zones when the munition is fired.
- Ensure the munition is properly aligned to the correct target aimpoint.
- Ensure that the Soldier performs misfire procedures correctly, or correct the problem.
- Signal to the tower operator when firers are ready to fire.
- Move firers on and off the firing line.
- Provide M18A1 claymore munition instruction.
- Demonstrate live-fire munitions.

Note. These personnel require no safety cards, but must be task-certified by their unit on all M18A1 claymore munition tasks.

Ammunition Personnel

4-40. The ammunition personnel are in charge of accountability and handing out M18A1 claymore munitions.

Note. The ammunition NCO must attend an ammunition handler's class provided by the local ammunition supply point (ASP).

Tower Operator

4-41. The tower operator controls Soldier movements during range operations and monitors communications with range control.

Guards

4-42. Guards control vehicle and foot traffic entering the range during range operations.

Medical Personnel

4-43. Medical support (with required medical supplies) must be present before and during range operations.

Truck Driver

4-44. The truck driver transports personnel to and from the range and provides support as needed (for example water, food, guard, and so forth).

TRAINING CONDUCT

4-45. Training conduct involves four steps:
(1) Occupy, inspect, and set up the range.
(2) Prepare for training.
(3) Conduct the training.
(4) Complete the training mission.

OCCUPY, INSPECT, AND SET UP THE RANGE

4-46. The OIC must establish communication with the installation's range control and request permission to occupy the range before personnel, materiel, or supplies arrive. Once this has been accomplished, the OIC and NCOIC should—
- Set up ammunition points and post guards.
- Establish locations for a medical station.
- Designate Soldier holding areas.

Chapter 4

- Establish water points.
- Designate parking areas.
- Inspect the range for operational conditions.
- Request an opening code from range control, if applicable.
- Raise the range flag.

PREPARE FOR TRAINING

4-47. The OIC and NCOIC should greet unit leaders and Soldiers as they arrive and direct them to the holding area. Actions at the holding area include the following:
- Ensure all Soldiers attending training have a helmet, a body armor vest, load-bearing equipment, and ear protection.
- Identify Soldiers to be trained.
- Conduct a safety briefing (to include administrative personnel).

CONDUCT THE TRAINING

Note. The OIC should monitor all training activities.

4-48. M18A1 claymore munition training covers those tasks learned during a Soldier's initial training, as well as unconventional employment procedures. During this phase of training, Soldiers receive instruction and perform hands-on training using an inert M18A1 claymore munition. This instruction covers the following tasks:
- Perform serviceability checks on an M18A1 claymore munition.
- Prepare an M18A1 claymore munition for firing.
- Demonstrate correct firing positions.
- Perform M18A1 claymore munition misfire procedures.
- Disarm the M18A1 claymore munition.
- Recover the M18A1 claymore munition.

Note. M18A1 claymore munition tasks should be taught or reinforced before conducting any form of live-fire training.

4-49. Trainers administer performance evaluations to determine how well Soldiers perform against established performance measures. Those who fail are retrained and retested, and those who pass help retrain and evaluate those who did not.

4-50. Tables 4-1 and 4-2 list the tasks, conditions, and standards for conventional employment and recovery of the M18A1 claymore munition.

Table 4-1. Task, conditions, and standards for employing the M18A1 claymore munition

TASK	Employ the M18A1 claymore munition.
CONDITIONS	1. Given an M18A1 claymore munition and a shock tube assembly with pull initiator, both packed in an M7 bandoleer; a sandbag; two wooden stakes; and a designated target area. 2. Given an M18A1 claymore munition, an M57 firing device, an M40 test set, and an M4 blasting cap assembly, all packed in an M7 bandoleer; a sandbag; two wooden stakes; and a designated target area.

STANDARD	Nonelectrical system (shock tube assembly with pull initiator):
	1. Employ the M18A1 claymore munition so that—
	   a. The front of the munition centers on a kill zone.
	   b. The igniter is 16 meters to the rear or side of the emplaced munition and is fired from a covered position.
	   c. The munition and shock tube are camouflaged.
	2. When the target is in the kill zone, fire the munition by pulling the igniter ring.
	Electrical firing system:
	1. Conduct a circuit test of the firing device, with the blasting cap secured under a sandbag.
	2. Employ the M18A1 claymore munition so that—
	   a. The front of the munition centers on a kill zone.
	   b. The firing device is 16 meters to the rear or side of the emplaced munition and is fired from a covered position.
	   c. The munition, firing wire, and firing device are camouflaged.
	   d. The installation is confirmed by conducting a final circuit test.
	3. When the target is in the kill zone, fire the munition by actuating the firing device handle with a firm, quick squeeze.

Table 4-2. Task, conditions, and standards for disarming and recovering the M18A1 claymore munition

TASK	Recover an M18A1 claymore munition.
CONDITIONS	1. Given an employed M18A1 claymore munition and a shock tube assembly with pull initiator, both packed in an M7 bandoleer; and a requirement to recover the munition. 2. Given an employed M18A1 claymore munition, an M57 firing device, an M40 test set, and a firing wire spool, all packed in an M7 bandoleer; and a requirement to recover the munition.
STANDARD	Disarm the M18A1 claymore munition without activating the munition, recover it, and repack all components into the M7 bandoleer.

COMPLETE THE TRAINING MISSION

4-51. At the completion of training, all equipment, range materiel, and ammunition should be accounted for, range maintenance should be completed, and the OIC and RSO should close the range. This includes the performing the following tasks:
- Request a closing code from range control.
- Release unit Soldiers.
- Remove all equipment and ammunition from the range.

Chapter 4

Note. Turn in all unexpended munitions to the ASP.

- Police the range, and perform other range maintenance as required by local SOP.
- Request a range inspection from range control when ready to clear.
- Turn in paperwork and equipment.
- Submit an after-action report to headquarters.
- Report any noted safety hazards to the proper authorities.

Chapter 5
Employment Considerations

Soldiers can use M18A1 claymore munitions in most situations where other types of munitions are employed, but they can also use them to cover the ranges between the maximum throwing distance for hand grenades and the minimum safe distance for mortar and artillery supporting fires.

USES

5-1. Soldiers use M18A1 claymore munitions for controlled firings, and nonstandard operation.

Note. Table 5-1 provides more information about the firing systems used for controlled firings.

CONTROLLED FIRINGS

5-2. For controlled firings, the Soldier observes the kill zone and detonates the munition as the forward edge of the enemy approaches a point within the kill zone where maximum casualties can be inflicted.

NONSTANDARD OPERATIONAL USE VERSUS STANDARD OPERATIONAL USE

5-3. Certain situations may require Soldiers to use additional devices to initiate M18A1 claymore munitions. For example, the situation could require more distance from the munition than the existing wire or shock tube allows, or the Soldier might need to fire multiple munitions.

Notes. 1. Table 5-1 provides more information about the firing systems that can be used for nonstandard and standard operation.

2. TM 9-1345-203-12 and FM 3-34.214 provide additional information about nonstandard operations.

Table 5-1. Firing systems, methods of initiation, and their uses

FIRING SYSTEM	METHODS OF INITIATION	USE	STANDARD/NONSTANDARD OPERATIONAL USE
Nonelectrical	Shock tube with pull initiator	Controlled	Standard operational use
	Time fuze attached to detonating cord with pull initiator	Both controlled and uncontrolled	Nonstandard operational use
Electrical	M4 blasting cap with M57 firing device	Controlled	Standard operational use

Chapter 5

FIRE DISCIPLINE

5-4. Since the M18A1 claymore munition can be fired only once, fire discipline is of paramount importance. Soldiers should not use the munition against single personnel targets; rather, they should use it against massed personnel. For controlled firings, the Soldier should not detonate the munition until the lead elements of an enemy formation come within 20 to 30 meters of the munition.

Note. Squad leaders or their superiors maintain responsibility for target selection and timely detonation.

CONTROLLED FRONTAL COVERAGE

5-5. For effective coverage of the entire front of a position, Soldiers must place munitions—
- In a line, no closer than 5 meters and no farther apart than 45 meters (Figure 5-1).

Note. The preferred lateral and rearward separation distance is 25 meters.

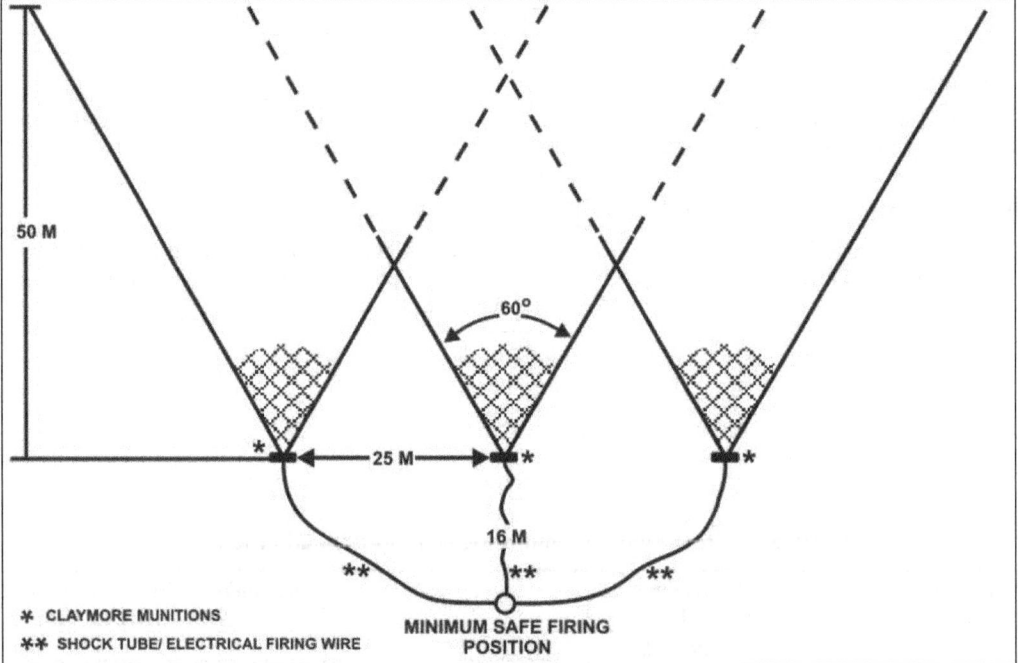

Figure 5-1. Diagram of lateral separation pattern

- In depth (from front to rear), no closer than 5 meters, provided that secondary missiles (debris) are removed.

Note. This distance prevents possible disturbance or damage to the rearward munitions.

OPERATIONS

5-6. Soldiers primarily use the M18A1 claymore munition as a defensive weapon; however, they can also use it during certain phases of offensive operations.

Note. The configuration and composition of the controlled dispersion pattern varies with the terrain and tactical situation.

DEFENSE

5-7. In defensive operations, Soldiers can use M18A1 claymore munition in the following ways:
- Controlled dispersion.
- Final protective fires.
- Security of outposts.
- Defense of command posts, support installations, and reserve forces.
- Roadblocks and obstacles.
- Retrograde operations.

Controlled Dispersion

5-8. Soldiers can also use M18A1claymore munitions alone or in multiples to cover areas where enemy personnel attacks are anticipated. Ease of installation and removal facilitates the use of M18A1 claymore munitions in protective, defensive, and nuisance usages (Table 5-2).

Table 5-2. Uses for controlled dispersion

USAGES	DETAILS
Protective	Soldiers employ M18A1 claymore munitions to supplement other munitions within a protective controlled dispersion pattern.
Defensive	Soldiers use M18A1 claymore munitions to cover portions of other defensive controlled dispersion munitions by emplacing them on the perimeter or within to cover lanes between munitions.

Final Protective Fires

5-9. Soldiers can use M18A1 claymore munitions to fill the dead space of the final protective fires of automatic weapons.

Notes.
1. Depending on the importance of the area being protected, Soldiers can choose to emplace multiple M18A1 claymore munitions behind each other in relatively close proximity, but no closer than five feet apart to avoid the risk of sympathetic detonation.
2. In determining positions for emplacing munitions, leaders consider the effects of backblast on friendly positions.

Security of Outposts

5-10. Soldiers can easily transport and rapidly emplace M18A1 claymore munitions to completely cover an outpost's perimeter and assist in covering withdrawals from outposts. Time permitting, several rows can be employed.

Defense of Command Posts, Support Installations, and Reserve Forces

5-11. Soldiers can use M18A1 claymore munitions to assist in the local security of command posts and support installations. Reserve forces in blocking positions or assembly areas can also use M18A1 claymore munitions to augment their local security forces.

> *Notes.* 1. When employing munitions in this way, Soldiers should use the controlled role to avoid inflicting casualties on friendly personnel.
>
> 2. Soldiers should mark, record, and report all such positions as described in FM 3-34.210.

Roadblocks and Obstacles

5-12. When used in conjunction with roadblocks, M18A1 claymore munitions should have clear fields of fire to cover avenues of approach. Soldiers should emplace additional munitions on the friendly side of a roadblock. When used to cover obstacles, the munition should be placed 20 to 30 meters on the friendly side of the obstacle.

> *Note.* When employing M18A1 claymore munitions for roadblocks, Soldiers should use the controlled role, since the operator can best judge the exact moment of detonation. When employing the munitions for obstacles, Soldiers can use the uncontrolled role; this allows the enemy to activate the munition when he attempts to breach the obstacle.

Retrograde Operations

5-13. M18A1 claymore munitions can be used during the following types of retrograde operations (Table 5-3):
- Delay.
- Withdrawal.
- Retirement.

Table 5-3. Types of retrograde operations

TYPE OF RETROGRADE OPERATIONS	DETAILS
Delay	The delaying unit could use the munitions in controlled roles to effectively attrit and delay the enemy.
Withdrawal	During a withdrawal, detachments left in contact can use emplaced M18A1 claymore munitions to cover the gaps left by the main force.
Retirement	Retirement operations are usually conducted when the unit is not in contact with the enemy. The security forces should use M18A1 claymore munitions to delay enemy movement that may interfere with the retiring unit.

OFFENSE

5-14. Attacking troops can easily transport the munition and use it for defending assembly areas, providing security during the conduct of the attack, and protecting the troops during the reorganization and consolidation of the objective. The M18A1 claymore munitions also provide an economical means for establishing effective ambushes.

Offensive Combat

5-15. The M18A1 claymore munitions can be employed in all phases of offensive combat (Table 5-4):
- Preparation for the attack.
- Conduct of the attack.
- Consolidation and reorganization.
- Defense of supporting elements during the attack.

Ambush

5-16. M18A1 claymore munitions provide an excellent, economical means for establishing effective ambushes deep in enemy territory with minimal use of friendly personnel. Small groups can easily transport a large number of munitions (for example, one man can carry six munitions, enough to cover a frontage up to 300 meters). M18A1 claymore munitions may be employed in the following ways (Table 5-5):
- Laterally, along the killing zone of the ambush, between the ambush element and the killing zone.
- At the front and rear of the killing zone.
- Laterally or at the front and rear of the killing zone, on the far side of the killing zone from the ambush element.
- Defiles.

5-17. Page 5-7 details the use of claymores in the ambush at Dak Po on 21-22 January 1969.

Table 5-4. Types of offensive combat

TYPES OF OFFENSIVE COMBAT	DETAILS
Preparation for the attack	A unit is particularly vulnerable to surprise enemy attacks as it approaches the enemy and occupies an assembly area prior to an attack. Soldiers can quickly emplace M18A1 claymore munitions around the perimeter of the assembly area to cover the unit during its preparation for the attack.
Conduct of the attack	Because M18A1 claymore munitions are easily employed and disarmed, flank security forces employ them during the conduct of the attack.
Consolidation and reorganization	During the conduct of the attack, assaulting troops may carry M18A1 claymore munitions for employment during reorganization and consolidation. After a unit has overrun an enemy position and pursued him by fire, it must immediately begin consolidation of the objective. Prompt emplacement of M18A1 claymore munitions provides the base for an immediate defense against possible counterattack. When the final objective is captured, Soldiers should immediately emplace the munitions.

Table 5-4. Types of offensive combat (continued)

TYPES OF OFFENSIVE COMBAT	DETAILS
Defense of supporting elements during the attack	Soldiers can use M18A1 claymore munitions in command posts or in the defense of supporting units, such as mortar and artillery batteries. As the first echelon of these supporting units moves into new positions, adequate defense measures should be established. M18A1 claymore munitions should be emplaced initially to cover likely avenues of enemy approach; eventually, they should be integrated with the fully developed defensive position. When displacements occur, Soldiers disarm the munitions, collect them, and move them to the next position. If other units occupy the area, the relieving unit and the displacing unit may agree for the munitions to be left in position. ***Note.*** When M18A1 claymore munitions are employed in the defense of command posts, supporting unit installations, or reserve forces in the rear of the battle positions, they must be well-marked and personnel should be familiarized with their location.

EXCERPTS FROM THE STAFF OF THE U.S. ARMY COMBAT STUDIES INSTITUTE REPORT
WANAT: COMBAT ACTION IN AFGHANISTAN, 2008

"By 12 July, [OP Topside] had become a complex of three interconnected fighting positions anchored by several large boulders that afforded an extra measure of protection. There was rising ground to the south and east and descending ground to the north and west. A large civilian compound stood about 100 yards to the southeast on higher ground. This location relinquished the ability to see into the nearby ravine to its north.

To offer greater protection from close threats, the paratroopers at [OP] Topside emplaced four M18A1 claymore command-detonated antipersonnel mines at the periphery of the dead ground to the east and the north, where the tree-filled ravine offered a particularly dangerous enemy avenue of approach. The operators positioned the mines after dark and recovered them at first light. The claymores at OP Topside were not dug into the ground, but simply placed on the ground inside the concertina wire and concealed with dirt and other debris.

[During the Battle of Wanat on 13 July 2008, a Soldier became pinned in OP Topside, with all of his comrades killed or wounded.] Out of weapons, [he] remembered that he still had two Claymore antipersonnel mines emplaced just outside the OP. A quick glance revealed that at least one insurgent had exploited the lapse in gunfire and emerged from the dead ground to the southeast to breach the concertina obstacle and assault the OP. Without hesitation, [he] detonated both mines, [killing the insurgent within the wire.]

[While other enemy casualties occurred during the battle,] only a single enemy corpse was recovered from the battlefield [at the battle's conclusion]. An American found the body of this insurgent in the concertina wire at the OP where he had become entangled. This is almost certainly the insurgent that [the Soldier] killed with his claymore."

Table 5-5. Types of ambush

TYPES OF AMBUSH	DETAILS
Laterally along the killing zone of the ambush, between the ambush element and the killing zone	This method of employment inflicts maximum damage on dismounted troops and provides a good counter to enemy immediate action drills, including assault into the ambush.
At the front and rear of the killing zone	This method of employment provides enfilade fire into the killing zones and greater economy of employment. It is particularly useful when the route through the killing zone is restricted in width. It also provides a good counter to enemy immediate action drills, including withdrawal or forward movement out of the killing zone along the original route.
Laterally or at the front and rear of the killing zone, on the far side of the killing zone from the ambush element	This method of employment provides a good counter to enemy immediate action drills, including maneuver or withdrawal out of the killing zone by moving away from the ambush element. *Note.* Soldiers must ensure that the ambush element is protected from the fragmentation of M18A1 claymore munitions.
Defiles	M18A1 claymore munitions are particularly effective in covering areas that might afford the enemy cover from small-arms fire, such as defiles. Soldiers can emplace munitions for ambushes on the ground, in trees, or on other upright objects which ensure a clear, unobstructed field of fire.

Glossary

Acronym/Term	Definition

A

AR	Army regulation
ARNG	Army National Guard
ARNGUS	Army National Guard of the United States
ASP	ammunition supply point

C

C4	composition 4 (explosive)

E

EOD	explosive ordnance disposal
environmental hazard	a condition with the potential for polluting air, soil, or water, or destroying cultural or historical artifacts

F

FM	field manual

M

MCOE	Maneuver Center of Excellence
METT-TC	mission, enemy, terrain and weather, troops and support available, time available, and civil considerations

N

NCOIC	noncommisisoned officer in charge

O

OIC	officer in charge

R

risk effect value	an indicator of the severity of environmental degradation
RSO	range safety officer

S

SDZ	surface danger zone
SOP	standard operating procedure

Glossary

Acronym/Term	Definition
	T
TADSS	Training Aids, Devices, Simulator, and Simulations
TM	technical manual
TRADOC	United States Training and Doctrine Command
TSC	training support center
	U
USAR	United States Army Reserve

References

SOURCES USED

These are the sources quoted or paraphrased in this publication. Army doctrinal publications and regulations are available online at: http://www.apd.army.mil.

AR 385-63, *Range Safety*, 30 January 2012.
DA PAM 385-63, *Range Safety*, 30 January 2012.
TC 3-21.75, *The Warrior Ethos and Soldier Combat Skills*, 13 August 2013.
FM 3-34.210, *Explosive Hazards Operations*, 27 March 2007.
FM 3-34.214, *Explosives and Demolitions*, 11 July 2007.
FM 5-19, *Composite Risk Management*, 21 August 2006.
TC 25-8, *Training Ranges*, 20 May 2010.
TM 9-1345-203-12, *Operator's and Unit Maintenance for Land Mines*, 30 October 1995.
TM 43-0002-33, *Destruction of Conventional Ammunition and Improved Conventional Munitions (ICM), to Prevent Enemy Use*, 15 November 1993.

DOCUMENTS NEEDED

These documents must be available to the intended users of this publication. DA Forms are available at http://www.apd.army.mil.

DA Form 2028, *Recommended Changes to Publications and Blank Forms*.

READINGS RECOMMENDED

These sources contain relevant supplemental information.
NONE.

WEBSITES

Most Army doctrinal publications and regulations are available online at: http://www.apd/army.mil. All other websites start here.
Army Knowledge Online (AKO): https://www.us.army.mil.
Central Army Registry (CAR) on the Army Training Network (ATN), https://atiam.train.army.mil.

This page intentionally left blank.

Index

A

aiming
  M57 firing device, 3-20
  shock tube assembly with pull initiator, 2-8
ambush, 5-5
  at the front and rear of the killing zone, 5-9
  defiles, 5-9
  example, 5-7
  laterally along the killing zone of the ambush, between the ambush element and the killing zone, 5-9
  laterally or at the front and rear of the killing zone, on the far side of the killing zone from the ambush element, 5-9
arming
  M57 firing device, 3-21
  shock tube assembly with pull initiator, 2-9

C

camouflaging
  M57 firing device, 3-24
  shock tube assembly with pull initiator, 2-15
capabilities, 1-1
circuit test
  final, 3-24
  initial, 3-8
command posts, defense of, 5-4
components, 1-1
  M57 firing device, 3-1
  shock tube assembly with pull initiator, 2-1
control measures, 4-4
  educational controls, 4-4
  physical controls, 4-4
controlled dispersion, 5-3
  defensive, 5-3
  protective, 5-3
controlled firings, 5-1
controlled frontal coverage, 5-2

D

danger areas, 1-3
defensive operations, 5-3
  controlled dispersion, 5-3
  defense of command posts, 5-4
  defense of reserve forces, 5-4
  defense of support installations, 5-4
  final protective fires, 5-3
  obstacles, 5-4
  retrograde operations, 5-4
  roadblocks, 5-4
description, 1-1
destroying
  M57 firing device, 3-30
  shock tube assembly with pull initiator, 2-28
disarming
  M57 firing device, 3-28
  shock tube assembly with pull initiator, 2-26

E

effects, 1-1
employing
  M57 firing device, 3-16
  shock tube assembly with pull initiator, 2-6
employment considerations, 5-1
environmental risk assessment, 4-5
  assess hazards, 4-5
  identify hazards, 4-5
equipment, 4-5

F

final protective fires, 5-3
fire discipline, 5-2
firing
  M57 firing device, 3-25
  shock tube assembly with pull initiator, 2-16
firing position
  M57 firing device, 3-7
  shock tube assembly with pull initiator, 2-5

I

instructors, 4-2
  duties, 4-3
  selection, 4-2

L

lateral separation pattern, 5-2

M

M57 firing device, 3-1
  components, 3-1
  operation under unusual conditions, 3-27
  standard operation, 3-7
methods of initiation, 1-2
  M57 firing device, 3-1
  shock tube assembly with pull initiator, 2-1
misfire
  M57 firing device, 3-27
  shock tube assembly with pull initiator, 2-18
misfire procedures
  type of mission, 2-18

O

obstacles, 5-4
offensive combat, 5-5
  conduct of the attack, 5-6
  consolidation and reorganization, 5-6
  defense of supporting elements during the attack, 5-7
  preparation for the attack, 5-6
offensive operations, 5-5
  ambush, 5-5
  offensive combat, 5-5
operation under unusual conditions
  M57 firing device, 3-27
  shock tube assembly with pull initiator, 2-18
operational use
  nonstandard, 5-1
  standard, 5-1
operations, 5-3
  defense, 5-3
  offense, 5-5

P

personnel, 4-6
  ammunition personnel, 4-7
  guards, 4-7
  medical personnel, 4-7
  noncommissioned officer in charge, 4-6
  officer in charge, 4-6, 4-7
  range safety officer, 4-7
  safety noncommissioned officers, 4-7

Index

truck driver, 4-7
Phase I training, 4-1
   elements, 4-1
   practical exercises, 4-1
Phase II training, 4-1
   elements, 4-2
   practical exercises, 4-2
phases of training, 4-1

R

range coordinations, 4-5
   equipment, 4-5
   personnel, 4-6
   ranges, 4-5
ranges, 4-5
recovering
   M57 firing device, 3-29
   shock tube assembly with pull initiator, 2-27
reserve forces, defense of, 5-4
retrograde operations, 5-4
   delay, 5-5
   retirement, 5-5
   withdrawal, 5-5
risk management process, 4-3
   assess hazards to determine risk, 4-4
   develop controls and make risk decisions, 4-4
   identify hazards, 4-3
   implement controls, 4-4
   supervise and evaluate, 4-5
roadblocks, 5-4

S

safety, 1-3
shock tube assembly with pull initiator, 2-1
   components, 2-1
   operation under unusual conditions, 2-18
   standard operation, 2-4
standard operation
   M57 firing device, 3-7
   shock tube assembly with pull initiator, 2-4
support installations, defense of, 5-4
surface danger zones, 4-4
sustainment training, 4-2

T

task, conditions, and standards
   disarming, 4-10
   employing, 4-10
   recovering, 4-10
technical specifications, 1-2
trainers, 4-2
   duties, 4-3
   selection, 4-2
training, 4-1
   aids, 4-2
   conduct, 4-8
   instructors, 4-2
   phases, 4-1
   preparation, 4-3
   range coordinations, 4-5
   sustainment, 4-2
   trainers, 4-2

training aids, 4-2
training conduct, 4-8
   complete the training mission, 4-11
   conduct the training, 4-8
   occupy, inspect, and set up the range, 4-8
   prepare for training, 4-8
   task, conditions, and standards for disarming, 4-10
   task, conditions, and standards for employing, 4-10
   task, conditions, and standards for recovering, 4-10
training preparation, 4-3
   environmental risk assessment, 4-5
   training risk assessment, 4-3
training risk assessment, 4-3
two methods to initiate detonation, 1-3

U

uses, 5-1
   controlled firings, 5-1
   controlled frontal coverage, 5-2
   fire discipline, 5-2
   nonstandard operational use, 5-1
   operations, 5-3
   standard operational use, 5-1

TC 3-22.23
15 November 2013

By Order of the Secretary of the Army:

RAYMOND T. ODIERNO
General, United States Army
Chief of Staff

Official:

GERALD B. O'KEEFE
Administrative Assistant to the
Secretary of the Army
1314210

DISTRIBUTION:

Active Army, Army National Guard, and U.S. Army Reserve: To be distributed in accordance with the initial distribution number (IDN) 116041 requirements for TC 3-22.23.

www.ingramcontent.com/pod-product-compliance
Lightning Source LLC
LaVergne TN
LVHW061346060426
835512LV00012B/2583